A Word to Live By

VOLUME 7
in the
**Church's
Teachings
for a
Changing
World**
series

LAUREN F. WINNER

Church Publishing
NEW YORK

Unless otherwise noted, the Scripture quotations contained herein are from the New Revised Standard Version Bible, copyright © 1989 by the Division of Christian Education of the National Council of Churches of Christ in the U.S.A. Used by permission. All rights reserved.

Church Publishing
19 East 34th Street
New York, NY 10016
www.churchpublishing.org

Cover art: "Lectio Divina," KPB Stevens, prayerbookart.com
Cover design by Laurie Klein Westhafer, Bounce Design
Typeset by Beth Oberholtzer

Library of Congress Cataloging-in-Publication Data

Names: Winner, Lauren F., author.
Title: A word to live / by Lauren Winner.
Description: New York, NY : Church Publishing, [2017] | Series: Church's
   teachings for a changing world series ; volume 7 | Includes
   bibliographical references and index.
Identifiers: LCCN 2017023200 (print) | LCCN 2017032728 (ebook) | ISBN
   9781640650008 (ebook) | ISBN 9780898692587 (pbk. : alk. paper)
Subjects: LCSH: Bible—Criticism, interpretation, etc. | Episcopal
   Church—Doctrines.
Classification: LCC BS511.3 (ebook) | LCC BS511.3 .W6625 2017 (print) | DDC
   220.6/1—dc23
LC record available at https://lccn.loc.gov/2017023200

Printed in the United States of America

Contents

Preface: An Acquired Taste   v

Chapter 1: What Are We Talking about When We
Talk about "The Bible"?   1

Chapter 2: Digesting Scripture   9

Chapter 3: On Genres   21

Chapter 4: The Liturgy of the Word   35

Chapter 5: Praying the Scriptures   47

Chapter 6: Life, Death, and Everything in Between   57

Chapter 7: Swimming in Scripture   69

Conclusion: Abundant, Inexhaustible   81

Acknowledgments   83

Notes   85

Preface
An Acquired Taste

"The Bible has been for me an acquired taste." That's the admission of the Episcopal priest and church historian Rowan Greer, offered early in his book *Anglican Approaches to Scripture*. Long after I'd forgotten everything Greer said about what sixteenth-century priests thought about the New Testament, I remembered his phrase: the Bible is an acquired taste.

I've lived most of my life in religious communities—first Jewish communities, then the Church of England, then the Episcopal Church—that encourage people to read the Bible. In all those communities, people listen to the Bible together at worship services, and people are encouraged to study the Bible in pairs or small groups, and to read Scripture alone, as part of their intimate life with God.

I was a very keen member of those communities—I was a practicing Jew, then a baptized Christian, then eventually ordained a priest in the Episcopal Church—yet the Bible bored me. I generally thought about other things when it came time to listen to a passage of Scripture in church on Sunday. I went to Bible study and enjoyed the potluck but found the study itself alternately tedious and alien. I tried to read the Bible at home alone, but I preferred reading the writings of Christian mystics, or novels about clergymen, or poems about the church year.

About seven years ago, however, something opened. It was a small opening, but a noticeable one—someone (the Holy Spirit, I think) walked over to a window that I'd thought was painted shut and jimmied it open a few inches. In those inches, I found myself open to and curious about the Bible. I found that, for the first time, I was particularly awake—to God and to myself—when I read the Bible. I began to have some inkling of what people mean when they say the Bible seems to effervesce with God's presence.

I still sometimes feel bored when I read the Bible, but now the boredom alternates with curiosity. I'm also often confused. But now I'm confused and *awake*.

PAUSE AND CONSIDER What are your feelings about the Bible? What are three adjectives you'd use to describe the Bible? Do you have any memories of encountering the Bible as a child? If so, what's the loveliest memory? What's the strangest or most uncomfortable memory?

• • •

Writing this book affected my spiritual life in two ways. First, it provoked a bit more of my own curiosity about Scripture. Once I began to organize my thoughts about the Bible into paragraphs and pages, I realized that many of my thoughts were really questions. Some of those questions—Why do Episcopalians read so much Scripture in church services? Does the Bible have a single narrative arc? What do Old Testament laws have to do with my life?—remain in these pages. Ruminating about them has been stimulating—the questions have stimulated my thinking and, I think, they've stimulated my friendship with the God to whom Scripture testifies and whose words Scripture gives.

Second, writing this book made me love Scripture more dearly. Peering closely at the Bible almost always does.

I hope that reading *A Word to Live By* will do the same for you—quicken your curiosity about the Bible, and help you love the Bible more dearly. A suggestion, then: read this book with a Bible nearby—on your computer or (my old-fashioned preference) leaves open on the sofa beside you. Reading *about* topics in Christian spiritual life—prayer, worship, friendship, Bible study—can take us deeply into the thing, but undertaking what we're reading about will carry us even further.*

In other words, reading the Bible both results from and is the agent of deeper curiosity about and perfected love of the Bible—so as you read this book, read the Bible too.

As you read the Bible, expect a few things.

Expect to be delighted.

Expect to be discomfited.

Expect to meet a few phrases you know, but didn't know as scriptural. Only recently did I realize that the phrase "eat, drink, and be merry" comes from the Bible; I think I dimly thought it was Shakespeare, but in fact you can find "eat, drink and be merry" in Ecclesiastes 8:15, and, in slightly shorter form, in Isaiah 22:13; centuries later, Paul used a version of the phrase in his first letter to the Corinthians.

---

* When you get to chapters four, five, and six, which consider some of the ways the Bible features in the Episcopal Church's worship services, you may want to have a Book of Common Prayer at hand too—find one at www.bcponline.org.

> Originally, the books of the Bible were not divided into chapters or into numbered verses. Today's chapter divisions are based on chapter breaks devised in the twelfth century by an English Roman Catholic bishop named Stephen Langton. Our verse breaks date to the fifteenth and sixteenth century. When you see a citation like "Ecclesiastes 8:15," the word before the numbers is the name of the biblical book in question, the number before the colon is the chapter, and the number following the colon is the verse.

Also, expect to be puzzled. Puzzlement is a good response to have to the Bible because the Bible is opaque, and puzzlement means you're paying attention to, rather than filtering out, the opaque bits. Some of the early church fathers said that the Bible is opaque *exactly so that we'd keep returning to it*; if it were straightforward and self-evident on the first or second pass, we'd move on to other texts.

> "The Bible . . . points beyond itself. It points to God."
> —*Verna Dozier*

Above all, expect to hear from God. Expect that God will speak to you through the Bible. To be sure, God can and does speak through other texts. Sometimes, God speaks to me through a friend. Sometimes, as the Bible itself suggests, God speaks to us through nature. But the Bible is the collection of texts through which, the church has discerned, God speaks to us most abundantly. And that, finally, is why we read it. Not because it's literarily stunning (though, in places, it is); not because it's hard to understand many English idioms and many works of Western literature if one doesn't have at least a passing familiarity with the stories of the Bible (though that's true). We read the Bible because we want to hear from God.

Chapter 1

What Are We Talking about When We Talk about "The Bible"?

At any Episcopal worship service, you will hear passages from the Bible. What, exactly, is the text from which we read in church? In this chapter, I'll try to answer that question by walking backwards, charting in reverse order the history of the biblical text.

When you hear the Bible read in an Episcopal church, you're usually hearing passages from the **New Revised Standard Version** of the Bible (often called, simply, the NRSV). That's a recent English translation of texts originally written in Hebrew, Aramaic, and Greek. The NRSV was published in 1989; it was produced by a group of scholars—mostly members of Protestant churches, though there were a few Catholic and Orthodox Christians, and one Jew. Their task was to update a 1952 translation of the Bible, the Revised Standard Version (RSV). In their work, which began in 1974, the NRSV translators set out to draw on the latest in biblical scholarship. They also wanted to update any passages that, because American idiomatic English had changed so much since 1952, sounded stilted to the 1970s ear, and they wanted to get rid of unnecessary masculine pronouns and to eliminate the words "man" and "men," if the Greek or Hebrew versions of those words didn't actually appear in the original (so the RSV's rendering of Matthew 6:30, "O men of little faith," became "you of little faith," and the RSV's "Man does not live by bread alone" in Matthew 4:4 became "One does not live by bread alone").

> Every new Bible translation has disgruntled critics. When the Revised Standard Version of the Bible was published in 1952, one minister in Rocky Mount, North Carolina, deemed the new translation "a heretical, communist-inspired Bible." He burned a copy with a blowtorch and sent the ashes to Luther Weigle, who'd chaired the translation committee.

The NRSV is by no means the only English translation of the Bible; on my bookshelf, I have nine different English translations, and even that is a small fraction of what's available. The Episcopal Church has authorized fourteen different translations for use in our worship services, but typically we read the NRSV. Most of the translations that Episcopalians can use in corporate worship were published in the last sixty years, but one is much older: the **King James Version** of the Bible (KJV), which was first printed in 1611, and which in some way stands behind all subsequent English translations. The King James was not the first English Bible—it was in part because there were so many different Bible translations floating around England at the beginning of the seventeenth century that James called for a new translation. (James hoped the new translation would be authoritative;

he also hoped it would replace the popular Geneva Bible, whose interpretative notes contained anti-monarchical sentiments.) It took several decades for the KJV to become established as the principal Bible in England; once it had, the KJV also began to predominate in the English colonies in North America.

So, we have a range of English translations—of what? Just what are these English texts, from the King James to the New Revised Standard Version, versions of?

The book known as the "**the Bible**"' is in fact a collection of over sixty books, which were themselves written over the course of perhaps one thousand years. We know with some confidence who wrote some of them (Paul's letter to the Galatians), and we don't know the authorship of others (the Psalms). It's long been thought that some material in the Bible was in circulation orally for many years before being written down; other biblical material was, in its first instantiation, a written text. By "books," I mean literary works with notional independence. A given biblical book was not necessarily written by one person, or even written at one time (Dorothy Sayers's novel *Thrones, Dominations* was completed after Sayers's death by Jill Patton Walsh; thus it has two authors, but it is one coherent work).

Over several centuries, early Christians discerned which books would constitute, and hold the authority of, sacred Scripture. The earliest Christians inherited—and continued to study and read in worship—Israel's Scripture, which comprised three sections: the Torah, the Prophets, and the Writings.

- The **Torah**—the five books of Moses—tells the story of the creation of the world, and God's relationship with humanity, focusing in particular on God's relationship with the descendants of Abraham and Sarah. The Torah follows those descendants, the people of Israel, into and out of slavery, and through a forty-year period in which they wandered in the desert, received a revelation of law from God, and made their way to the edge of the land of Canaan.

- The **Prophets** are collections of oral declamations by people chosen by God to speak to the people of Israel, to interpret their present to them, to remind them to keep God's law, and to chart a vision for their future.

- The **Writings** encompass poems, prayers, proverbs, narratives about individual men and women's faith lives, and histories.

The Torah, the Prophets, and the Writings were originally written in Hebrew and Aramaic. By the time Jesus was born, various Jewish communities had translated the Hebrew and Aramaic texts into Greek, the dominant language of politics, trade, and learning in much of the Mediterranean world. The earliest Christians read these Greek translations alongside Hebrew and Aramaic texts of the Jewish scriptures, especially as the church spread among Jews and Gentiles for whom Greek was a mother tongue. (By custom, these various Greek translations of scriptural books are referred to as the **Septuagint**. The term "Septuagint" comes from the Latin for "seventy"; the term was applied to the Greek Jewish scriptures because it was thought that 70 Jewish scholars translated the books of Moses into Greek in Alexandria some time in the third century BCE.)

As the first Christians were continuing to read and study Israel's Scripture, they were also producing their own literature and reading it in church. Letters of theological instruction and practical counsel, written by Paul of Tarsus, circulated throughout the churches, and Gospels (accounts of the events leading up to and following the death of Jesus of Nazareth) began circulating, and other texts circulated, too. By the middle of the second century CE, Christians began discerning with focused intentionality which of these new texts should be read in church worship and studied in church. They were trying to clarify which letters and Gospels Christians absolutely needed to read, which texts Christians urgently needed to converse with, and which texts could confidently be known to convey the words of God to God's people.

That discernment entailed real debate. In particular, there were arguments about whether to include the epistle to the Hebrews and the Revelation of John of Patmos. These arguments turned largely on three questions.

1. Early Christians asked whether the content of the books was consistent with what they knew about God.

2. They were also interested in who had written the text—was it written by someone who had witnessed personally the events he was writing about, or who was otherwise deemed a trustworthy reporter?

3. And finally, early Christians wanted to know whether there was consensus among Christian communities that a given book was life-giving, inspired, and inspiring. Did Christian communities generally agree that a book helped their faith grow and helped them follow Jesus? St. Jerome, for example, said that it didn't much matter that no one knew who wrote the letter to the Hebrews, because the letter was "constantly read in the churches."

By the end of the fourth century, the churches in the Roman Empire had settled on the books that they understood to be the words of the Lord and therefore to be read in church and studied for interest and edification. To the Jewish scriptures, the church had added the Gospels according to Matthew, Mark, Luke, and John; a text called Acts of the Apostles, which recounts the ministries of several early Christians who were crucial in spreading the story of Jesus throughout the Roman Empire; twenty-one letters; and the Revelation of John of Patmos. (They'd settled not only on which texts to embrace as Scripture; they'd also affirmed the importance of the order I just gave, the same order you'll find in the table of contents of any New Testament today.)

PAUSE AND CONSIDER How do you respond to this history— to the Bible's comprising a collection of books written over many centuries, whose status as "biblical" required discernment and debate?

The early Christians' long discernment concluded the process of **canon formation**, and the books finally included in the small library we know as the Bible are called the biblical **canon**. It's a basic component of Christian faith to think that the Holy Spirit worked through the early Christians in this process of canon formation. The church has always affirmed that Christians can read, and expect to be spiritually edified and theologically nurtured by, books that aren't included in Scripture. But Scripture alone is the text we proclaim in worship and respond to in sermons. And Scripture alone is the text about which Christians say "these are the words by which God speaks directly to us."

Canons are, it must be admitted, somewhat out of fashion. Fifty years ago, it seemed to people that there was a clear "canon of Western literature" and "canon of Western art." Today, not only the scope of those canons is debated; the very sense that we can meaningfully talk about a canon of Western literature, or should want to, has been usefully subjected to scrutiny by people

> Roman Catholic editions of the Bible have seventy-three books; all Protestants, including Episcopalians, include only sixty-six. The extra (or, depending on your perspective, missing) books were included in some, but not all, ancient Jewish collections of Scriptures. In antiquity and the Middle Ages, Christians understood the books in question to be part of the Bible, even as there were learned Christians who questioned their status because the books were not included in all Jewish scriptural collections. During the sixteenth century, Protestants affirmed that (in the phrasing of Martin Luther) these books "are not held equal to the Sacred Scriptures and yet are useful and good for reading," while Catholics affirmed the books as "sacred" and canonical. The Episcopal Church acknowledges them as (in the words of one sixteenth-century Anglican) "read for example of life and instruction of manners," and we occasionally read passages from some of them—Judith, Baruch, Sirach, and the Wisdom of Solomon—during worship.

who are interested in giving Tabitha Tenney's 1799 novel *Female Quixotism* (a novel I adore) or Harriet Jacob's 1860 autobiography *Incidents in the Life of a Slave Girl* (which I read annually) the same attention they accord *Moby-Dick*.

So why a biblical canon? I sometimes chafe against our canon. I think it would be interesting to preach on one of the gospels that was excluded from our biblical library, and there are bits of Ezekiel and Ephesians I'd like to skip. But I believe that, just as Jacob wrestled with the angel and was eventually blessed by his wrestling (Genesis 32:22–31), the task given to us by the early church's canon formation is a task of committed wrestling.

I needn't understand or enjoy or feel affinity for all of Scripture—but I'm committed to wrestling with it, and I believe that eventually, I'll be blessed by that wrestling (though I also think the wrestling might leave me, as it left Jacob, limping).

In my canon-wrestling, I sometimes muse about etymology. "Canon" comes from the Greek word for "rule." The Greek word is a Semitic language word adopted into Greek; the Semitic word means "ruler" or "measuring rod," and it, in turn, comes from a Semitic root that designates a "reed"; that root is etymologically related to "cane," as in sugar cane. Historically, the reason we began to call the books of the Bible our "canon" is that the list of canonical books constitutes a rule for our reading, and the books in question constitute a rule of faith. No one was thinking about sugar cane when they began to speak of the biblical canon. But I like to think of it. Sugar cane has a complicated history—its history in the West is inseparable from the history of slavery, and the history of poverty in the Caribbean. There's a bitterness to sugar cane, just as there is bitterness to how biblical texts have, in history, sometimes been used to violent ends.

But sugar cane, like the canon, is sweet. In the words of the Bible itself, "How sweet are your words to my taste, sweeter than honey to my mouth" (Ps. 119:103).

PAUSE AND CONSIDER Scripture brims with similes, metaphors, and other flights of prose that help us see what kind of book Scripture is. According to various biblical books, Scripture is a lamp, a running path, a blanket of snow on the landscape, a mirror. Which of these metaphors intrigue you? If the Bible is a running path, where does it lead? If the Bible is a mirror, what should we expect to see when we read the Bible?

appointed for that Sunday. In that reading, Paul assures the fledging church in Rome that Scripture "was written in former days . . . for our instruction, so that by steadfastness and by the encouragement of the scriptures we might have hope" (Romans 15:4). The collect that people prayed a few minutes before hearing those words is now known as "the collect for Scripture." In the prayer, we ask God to allow us to hear the Scriptures, and to "read, mark, learn, and inwardly digest them."

Whenever I hear or say the collect for Scripture, I am struck by the word "digest." I like the image of chewing the Bible, digesting it, metabolizing it. Throughout the centuries, Christians have spoken of eating the Bible. It's a metaphor that captures how hungry we are (or ought to be) for what's inside Scripture; how singularly Scripture nourishes us; and how delicious Scripture is. "Taste the goodness of your Redeemer," wrote Anselm of Canterbury in the eleventh century. "Chew the honeycomb of his words, suck their flavor, which is more pleasing than honey, swallow their health-giving sweetness. Chew by thinking, suck by understanding, swallow by loving and rejoicing." Anselm was echoing language found in Scripture itself: the prophet Jeremiah speaks of finding God's words and eating them, whereupon they became the delight of his heart. (Jeremiah 15:16) and the prophet Ezekiel had a vision in which he was commanded to eat a scroll inscribed with words of mourning and woe; when he ate it, he found that "in my mouth it was as sweet as honey" (Ezekiel 2:9–3:3). The Book of Common Prayer, alas, is a tad more restrained than Anselm, but nonetheless gustatory: read, mark, learn, and inwardly digest the words of the Bible.

As a verb, "digest" means to break down food so that your body can absorb its nutrients, and it means to ponder something, or think it through. "Digest" was a noun before it was a verb, though; as a noun, it means a summary or condensed version of a literary or historical work—hence, the magazine *Reader's Digest*.

A few years ago, in an effort to take seriously the collect's hope that we might all "digest" the Scriptures, I started writing down summaries, or digests, of Scripture. I do this every few months: I sit down and scratch out a summary of a biblical book, or of the Bible as a whole. This is a way of becoming close to the Bible. It's like sitting in front of a painting in a museum, and drawing a sketch of the painting you see—it requires attending to, and growing in love of, the thing you're sketching. The very act of making such a sketch or summary reminds me that sketching a beautiful thing, or summarizing a beautiful text, will never fully or adequately render the object of my sketch. Summarizing a biblical text also shows me something about myself, about my predilections and questions and biases: Where does my eye go? What holds my interest?

Herewith a short digest of Scripture—it's inadequate, as any summary would be, and it tells you as much about the summarizer and her interests as it does about the Scriptures themselves. But it might helpfully orient your own reading of Scripture, and it might prompt you to offer your own digest thereof.

A First Digest

In the beginning, God created. That's the beginning of the Bible—a poetic account of God's creating the cosmos, the planets, moons, tortoises, rose bushes, barnacles, squid. People are created, too—in the "image" and "likeness" of God (Genesis 1:26–27).

PAUSE AND CONSIDER Read Genesis 1:1–2:4. Then, take out a sheet of paper and write—for ten minutes, without stopping—your answer to this question: why did God create the world?

The Bible's account of creation shows God's love and desire for variety, for life, for creatures to love. That desire and love overflows and creates all that is and, as Genesis tells us, that creation is good. That's what the first two chapters of the Bible are devoted to: creation; God's abounding love; creation's goodness.

And then, in the very next chapter (Genesis 3), that good creation becomes deeply damaged. This is the story of the serpent, of Adam and Eve's eating from the fruit of the tree of knowledge of good and evil. This story is often called, in Christian speech, the story of **the Fall**, because the story depicts Adam and Eve falling away from God. The Bible doesn't sugarcoat this Fall or its effects; indeed, the Bible is up front about death and suffering; from here on, all of creation will know violence and anguish, and the rest of the Bible will depict that anguish.

It will also depict God's ongoing healing of all that God created: God's slow, local interventions, which intertwine death with life and suffering with joy. And the rest of the Bible is also threaded with the hope for **redemption**—the hope that one day, all the damage will be completely healed, and there will be no violence or suffering or death. As the very last book of the Bible predicts, in the fullness of time, God "will wipe every tear from their eyes. Death will be no more; mourning and crying and pain will be no more" (Revelation 21:4). Indeed the Bible depicts that healing as a new creation, and names Jesus, the agent of that new creation, as a new Adam (1 Corinthians 15:42–49). A particularly stirring depiction of that new creation is found in Isaiah 65, where God declares: "For I am about to create new heavens and a new earth." In that new creation, earlier sufferings "shall not be remembered or come to mind," and the kinds of horrors that have occurred since the Fall will have no place in that new creation—"No more shall there be in it an infant that lives but a few days, or an old person who does not live out a lifetime," thus "no more shall the sound of weeping be heard in it, or the cry of distress." Even animals who, in our fallen world, must kill one another to survive will be friends: "The wolf and the lamb shall feed together, the lion shall eat straw like the ox."

Theologians like to say that God's original creation was perfect—yet the new, redeemed creation will be better than the original creation. They ground this idea in part in biblical passages that suggest that the city God will build at the end of time will be more wonderful than the original Jerusalem (see Haggai 2:6–9). The book of Job also suggests that God's redeemed creation is more perfect than the original creation. Job has lost everything—his livelihood is destroyed and all of his animals and children have died. For many chapters, Job talks with his friends about his losses, and then for a few more chapters, Job hears directly from God; in particular, he hears from God about God's creation of creation, God's having created and every day sustained thunderbolts and ostriches and mountain goats and stars. And then, at the very end of the book, we read that Job had more children—seven sons and three daughters. The daughters, the text tells us, were more beautiful than anyone in the land. And the daughters' names? Job named them Dove, Cinnamon, and Horn of Eye-Shadow. What have Job and his daughters to do with God's final healing of the world? Only this: when God made a new creation for Job—when God gave Job new daughters—those daughters were more excessive in their beauty and splendor than the perfectly beautiful and splendid original daughters. We aren't, I think, meant to infer that these new daughters make up for the sons and daughters that died— as much as any other biblical book, Job doesn't evade loss with bromides. Rather, Dove, Cinnamon, and Horn-of-Eye-Shadow show us that all the horror of death and loss will eventually be transfigured into something inexplicably better: the splendors of God's new creation will be even more remarkable than the splendors of untouched Eden.

But we're getting ahead of ourselves. Creation's fall from intimacy with God occurs in the third chapter of Genesis, and then, in the next few chapters of the Bible, violent things happen—a man murders his brother, for example, and overall "every inclination of the thoughts of their hearts was only evil continually" (Genesis 6:5). These violences and evil inclinations show us, in one way or another, that humanity (and indeed all of creation) is no longer in a state of intimate, perfect communion with God. In fact, we're estranged from God and from one another, so much so that I might become so jealous of my brother's relationship with God that I kill him. The Bible, then, is straightforward in its depiction of the bleak and painful aspects of existence. But it also shows that, at our worst, we still have some of our God-given goodness; before he's murdered, Abel makes a delightful gift to God; most of humanity is shot through with evil desire, but Noah and his family are pleasing enough to God that God spares them in the flood. So the insistence in Genesis 1 that human beings are made in God's image turns out to be quite significant—even at our cruelest and most depressed, we still bear the likeness of God.

When I read these early chapters of Genesis, I feel that I am in a mythical world of fairy-tale truths so exaggerated that I can't possibly miss them. The Bible is taking pains to show us that, having fallen away from God, people are lost and violent and alienated from God and one another; even so, this is not a completely bleak and charred world.

Beginning in Genesis 9, and continuing through the rest of Scripture, is a series of invitations: over and over, God invites people to dwell with God, and the people give varied responses to these invitations. First, in Genesis 9, God invites all of humanity to dwell in some modicum of peace with God and with one another—this is known as the "Noahide **covenant**," because it is an invitation God makes to all of humanity through Noah and his descendants. (The form of this—an invitation extending through one person to many generations of people yet unborn—is, I think, hard to grasp, because it's so different from the patterns of today's highly individualistic society. It's a bit like one person endowing a scholarship at a university—that's a gift, or invitation, given through one institution, with the intent of blessing generations to come.) The Noahide covenant shows God's love for all of humanity, and shows God's choice to enter into a relationship of intimacy with all people.

Then God makes a series of invitations to one specific group of people—the descendants of Abraham and Sarah. The invitations and promises God makes to the children of Abraham and Sarah is known as "the **election** of Israel." ("Israel" is one of the names given to Abraham and Sarah's grandson, who is also called Jacob. When we speak of the election of Israel, we mean that as a synecdoche—not that God elected only the man Jacob/Israel, but that God elected all of Jacob's descendants, and knit them into a people called Israel.) God chooses, or elects, Israel to be in particularly intimate relationship with God, and God says that through this relationship, God will heal not only the people of Israel of their damage; somehow, mysteriously, God will heal all of creation through God's love of Israel.

The election of Israel is one of the most confusing things that God does (and theologians say that the very fact that election is confusing ought to remind us that God is wildly free from our expectations about how a god should act). Why does God choose to heal the world of its damage through one particular group of people? And on what basis did God choose Israel, and not, say, North Carolinians or the Quebecois? Scripture isn't interested in answering those questions; it's more interested in telling stories about Israel than in theorizing about why God chose to work through Israel. But through those stories, we can see one pronounced, indisputable characteristic of God: God doesn't heal the world by grand, cosmic gestures from on high. Rather, God chooses to heal by particular intimacy. The election of Israel, in other words, shows us something about how God's love works: it doesn't wash over the world in an equally distributed bath. It enters the world locally and spreads out. God's presence and healing balm is, paradoxically, present everywhere yet not equally distributed. This is part of why the idea of election is confusing—God's focus on one group of people can seem capricious and arbitrary, even mean. But the end to which the election of Israel points is not, simply, God's intimacy with Israel. Rather, the election of Israel is a path that God walks into intimacy with everyone and every created being.

God elects Israel for particular intimacy, and in that election Scripture shows us that God heals by local intimacy. But then Scripture shows us something more: Several hundred years after being elected for this particular intimacy with God, the people of Israel are enslaved in Egypt: "The Egyptians became ruthless in imposing tasks on the Israelites, and made their lives bitter with hard service in mortar and brick and in every kind of field labor. They were ruthless in all the tasks that they imposed on them" (Exodus 1:13–14). Israel's being enslaved just a few generations after God establishes particular intimacy with Israel makes clear that intimacy with God doesn't inoculate from harm or suffering.

And then, after recounting Israel's enslavement, the Bible depicts God's liberating Israel from slavery. With this account of slavery and liberation, the text discloses a pattern that recurs throughout Scripture. The pattern has four steps: People suffer; God hears the groans of suffering; God liberates the people from the condition of suffering; God makes another invitation to the people. In this case, Israel is enslaved; God hears Israel's groaning; God comes down from the heavens and liberates Israel from bondage in Egypt—and then makes another invitation of intimacy to Israel in the form of the laws that God reveals to Israel on Mt. Sinai. Those laws, which turn the very practices of eating and dressing and hiring and working and marrying and mourning and counting and harvesting into means of looking at God, fill large sections of Exodus, Leviticus, Numbers, and Deuteronomy.

The next time we see the pattern, the topic is land. God gives Israel the land of Canaan to live in. After wandering in the desert for forty years, the people arrive in that land. With slaughter that can (indeed, should) be difficult to read about, they take possession of the land and establish themselves there. For a season, the people are ruled by judges, who, with a few notable exceptions such as Deborah, are not skilled leaders. The people forget what they once knew about God, and they give themselves over almost wholly to violence.

Eventually, the people decide they want to be governed, as neighboring peoples are, by a king. God tells them this is not a good idea, because a monarchy will inevitably raise questions about where Israel's primary allegiance lies, but the people insist that they really, really want a king. So God gives them a monarchy, and the third monarch, Solomon, builds the temple.

For a while, it seems that perhaps the four-fold pattern is broken: perhaps the people will find a way of dwelling with God in the land that God gave them under the rule of wise (if decidedly imperfect) kings like David and Solomon. But the pattern endures—the people are swept into **exile**. Partial exile begins in the eighth century BCE and comes to a head in 586 BCE, when the

Babylonians conquer Jerusalem. The temple is destroyed, and many of the Jewish people living in and around Jerusalem were taken into exile in Babylon. They had little reasonable hope of ever returning to their homeland.

> "BCE" and "CE." "BCE" stands for "Before the Common Era" and "CE" stands for "during the Common Era." These terms, which were first used in the nineteenth century, are non-confessional ways of designating the same eras that "BC" ("Before Christ") and "AD" ("*Anno Domini*," or "In the Year of Our Lord") designate; that is, both indicate use of the Gregorian calendar, whose pivotal point is the birth of Jesus of Nazareth.

This exile is the context for a large chunk of the Old Testament. Much of the second half of the book of Isaiah, for example, is taken up with attempting to reassure the exiles that, although it appears that God has totally abandoned them, in fact God remains faithful to them and is working, in ways they cannot see, for their redemption. The book of Daniel depicts a person in exile resisting his captors. Psalm 137 declares that in Babylon, the people sat down by the river and wept for their homeland. In Jeremiah 29, God tells the exiles not only to pine for home, but also to build houses and plant gardens, to get married and have families, and to "seek the welfare of the city where I have sent you into exile, and pray to the LORD on its behalf, for in its welfare you will find your welfare" (Jeremiah 29:7).

The exiles remain in captivity until 538 BCE, when the Babylonian emperor Cyrus allows them to return home; in waves over several decades, many of the exiles return (those waves of return are recounted in the biblical books Ezra and Nehemiah), whereupon they build a new temple in the spot where the first temple had stood.

This experience of exile was akin to slavery—the people were lost and suffering. And just as God heard the groanings of Israel in slavery and liberated them, so God heard Israel's groaning in the exile, and returned them to their land, whereupon God made a new offer of intimacy in the form of a return to the land and a rebuilt temple. This second temple is the one that is still standing during Jesus's lifetime. Much changes politically between the time the exiles return to the land in the late sixth century and the birth of Jesus—Persian political control of the land gives way to Hellenistic political control, and, by the time Mary and Joseph are toddling around, Hellenistic political control has given way to Roman rule. But the temple still stood. It is in this second temple that the infant Jesus is presented to God and spied by an awe-filled, poetic old man named Simeon; it is in this temple that Jesus hangs out, as a boy, studying Scripture with the rabbis; it is from this temple that Jesus expels salesmen and money-changers; it is this temple that Jesus refers to as "my Father's house"; it is this temple that Jesus, quoting Isaiah, says will be a house of prayer for all nations.

God invites Israel into intimacy through a reestablishment of Israel in their land and through a second temple. And then, in the New Testament, God enters into profound intimacy with Israel, and ultimately with other people too, through becoming incarnate in the person of Jesus of Nazareth.

In this **incarnation** we see a clarification and intensification of three themes that have run throughout Scripture. First, Jesus is a concentrated invitation to intimacy: laws and temples were channels through which the people of Israel could reach God, but in the incarnation, God is right there, walking around among the people.

Second, the incarnation is an intensification of the particularity of election. God comes to the world as a Jew; that is, God comes to the world as person who is a member of the community God so long ago elected for intimacy. Jesus is an intensification of God's preference for working out salvation through local particulars—God first elected a particular people, and then God came to us as a particular person. To put that differently, the election of Israel tends toward Jesus, and in Jesus, we see, in concentrated form, God's choice to work out the healing of everyone through intimacy with Israel.

Third, in Jesus, we see, again, that intimacy with God does not inoculate. Echoing election-then-slavery, and land-then-exile, Jesus of Nazareth is killed. And then (echoing after-slavery-liberation and after-exile-return), God restores Jesus through resurrection, and makes a new offer of intimacy to people through the establishment of the church, through the presence of the Holy Spirit, and through the gift of the Eucharist.

A Second Digest

Here's an even more compressed digest of Scripture: God creates a world of beautiful silver—teapots and ice tongs and butter knives and aspic forks. The silver wrestles itself away from God's care into the open air, and gets tarnished. God is in the kitchen, polishing the silver.

Chapter 3

On Genres

The Bible contains a diversity of genres. I first learned this shortly after being baptized—I was maybe twenty-two—when I stumbled across a book called *How to Read the Bible for All Its Worth* by Gordon D. Fee (a New Testament scholar) and Douglas Stuart (an Old Testament scholar). In the preface to that book, Fee and Stuart wrote, "[T]he basic concern of this book is with the different types of literature (the *genres*) that make up the Bible. . . . We affirm that there is a real difference between a psalm, on the one hand, and an epistle on the other." Because Fee and Stuart believe that "these differences are vital and should affect . . . the way one reads," they aim to help Christians read the psalms as poems, the epistles as letters, and so forth.

Fee and Stuart's argument was elementary, but I was electrified by it. I could immediately see that this basic insight would fundamentally shape how I read the Bible, and I didn't have to possess special biblical knowledge to understand what Fee and

Stuart were getting at; I understood them because my own book-shelves held many genres—cookbooks, history books, poetry, novels, memoirs, travel guides—and it wouldn't make much sense to read *The Joy of Cooking* in the same way that I read Emily Dickinson's elusive verse.

Fee and Stuart helped me see that I already knew more than I realized I knew about how to read the Bible. Yes, there are some differences between letters written in the first century and letters written today, but there are also some similarities. Paul's letters to churches in Rome and Philippi were easier to read and more interesting once I saw that they were first *letters*, and only second (if at all) gnomic instructions for living the good life. That they were letters meant, foremost, that they aimed to reconnect people who were separated by physical distance; Paul wasn't just promulgating rules; he was also making overtures of love to people he cared about but was physically far away from. Insofar as Paul did give instructions, those instructions were written to particular communities who were in the middle of sorting out particular problems.

Fee and Stuart also showed me that the Bible isn't all one thing: it's not all a legal code. It's not all a historical account. And it certainly isn't a science book. (I can remember sitting in my bedsit with Fee and Stuart, and instantly realizing that if the Bible comprised many genres, and if the Genesis account was a poem or a founding myth, then reading the first few chapters of Genesis like a biology textbook was wrongheaded, and people's dramas over the seeming contradiction between the six days of creation and Darwin misplaced.)

Genre conventions are hints that texts give us about how the texts want to be read. When I read a sonnet—a fourteen-line poem that makes a thematic or dictional turn, usually in the second half of the poem—I know to be on the lookout for the turn.

When I pick up a mystery novel, I know that part of my readerly task is to figure out whodunit. Of course, that genre-specific task isn't exhaustive of the mystery novel: when reading a sophisticated mystery novel, I'll also get to know complex characters and see the world as they see it; encounter strong articulations of values I may or may not share; and be taken to a location I've not visited in real life (or, as when I read Margaret Maron's mysteries, set in piedmont North Carolina and New York City, be shown things I may or may not already know about places I've lived for years).

Similarly, knowing that there are genres in the Bible can lead us to ask what the genre of a particular biblical text we're reading is, and what that genre is trying to do for its reader.

PAUSE AND CONSIDER Brainstorm a list of the books in your house, or the books on your Kindle, or the books that you've read at least part of over the last year. Then group those books into categories: novels, cookbooks, journalistic explorations of current events, hymnals, prayer books, volumes of letters, poems, self-help books, and so on. Then, jot down a few aspects that make each category distinctive: What are authors of each genre trying to do? What are you looking for when you read in each genre? Do the different genres assume the reader has any specialized knowledge before she picks up the book? What would your reading experience be if you picked up a self-help book expecting it to be a novel?

Biblical books don't always fit neatly into genres, but here are a few of the categories I've found helpful in reading the Bible (my discussion is by no means comprehensive). I'll begin by discussing genres principally associated with the Old Testament, and then look at genres associated with the New.

Some of the Bible's Genres

The Bible opens (Genesis 1–3) with a **founding narrative**, which we often refer to as "the creation story." All institutions and communities have founding narratives: countries tell founding narratives (brave colonists rallying around "taxation without representation"); companies tell them (Apple lore begins with Steve Jobs in his parents' garage); even families (my grandparents' elopement, almost thwarted by a torrential rainstorm). These founding narratives codify in a story what matters most to a community.

Another major genre of the Bible is **laws**. Just as our own society is organized around legal codes, so ancient Israel lived in response to various laws. Old Testament laws govern all manner of topics: how to treat economically marginal people and how to welcome strangers, what foods are permissible to eat, what fabrics you can use to make your clothes, when to work and when to rest, how to interact with your employees, when to make certain offerings and supplications to God, how to observe the new moon, who can marry whom, what punishments a murderer or adulterer should incur.

I love immersing in a long passage of biblical laws—though I realize it is precisely those passages (in, say, Leviticus and Deuteronomy) where many well-meaning Christian readers of the Bible get bogged down and bored, and decide it would be more profitable to read a magazine. I love the laws because through them, the people of Israel drew near to God. The laws, in other words, represent conscious bids for holiness in the midst of everyday life, and they suggest that no part of life is separate from our life with God. As the Christian ethicist Stanley Hauerwas has put it, "Any God who won't tell you what to do with your pots and pans and genitals isn't worth worshipping."

Increasingly, I find myself wondering about *reputation* when I read Old Testament laws. What would the reputation of a community who followed these laws be? What would that community be known for? For example, a community that observed the Old Testament laws governing treatment of strangers and aliens might be known as riskily generous. A community that observed the Old Testament dietary codes might be known as a community that recognized the complexities of human appetites and that was interested in limits. As Christians, we don't observe the letter of most of the Old Testament laws, but we might want to be known for the same sorts of things. And we can then ask, what sorts of practices might we adopt so that we can likewise have a reputation of extravagant generosity and awareness of appetite and limit?

A third important genre is **history**. Histories—books like I and II Samuel, I and II Kings, I and II Chronicles—tell stories of the past; they hold Israel's social and cultural memory. The Bible retells these stories not simply to say "this is what happened," but also to offer a theological statement about what happened—to identify God's role in history, and to suggest God's perspective on history. Today's world is, of course, in many ways different from, say, the tenth century BCE (when David was king). But many of the questions the historical books consider are still before us today: How shall we govern ourselves? How should we organize ourselves militarily and what kinds of military actions do we undertake? How should societies treat the economically marginal members of their communities? And how do we discern God's desires, rather than just make our own decisions, in the midst of such questions?

Readers of the Old Testament also encounter **psalms**. The Bible's 150 psalms are poems, and most of them are songs, and most of them are prayers. The word "psalm" comes from a Greek word that means "the twitching of a harp string." When we pray the psalms, we become a musical string twitching, and the words of the psalms are the notes.

Note the verb: we can, of course, "read" the **Psalter** (the collected set of psalms), but the psalms deeply want to be prayed.
Most of them are addressed directly to God, and they express
to God almost every imaginable human emotion. Some of the
psalms wail with lament, some shout with praise and thanksgiving, some seethe with anger and ask God to destroy the psalmist's (or pray-er's) enemies. Athanasius, a fourth-century bishop,
wrote that within the Psalter "are represented and portrayed in
all their great variety the movements of the human soul. It is
like a picture in which you see yourself portrayed, and seeing,
may understand and consequently form yourself upon the pattern given. . . . You find depicted in it all the movements of your
soul, all its changes, its up and down, its failures and recoveries.
In fact, in all the circumstances of life, we shall find that these
divine songs meet our own souls' need at every turn."

The psalms suggest to us that the posture human beings
should take to God is the posture of *exposure*. We can and should
take our terror, our rage, our anguish, our doubt, our adulation,
our ecstasies, our awe to God. At the same time, the very fact
that Scripture gives us psalms to pray suggests that we ought not
always, and perhaps we ought only secondarily, formulate our
exposures on our own. I might be in the grip of anger or desola-
tion or ardor, and the best way to speak that ardor or anguish
turns out not to be my own crumpled sentences; the best way to
speak the ardor or the awe is supplied, in the psalms, by the One
I wish to speak it to. Thus, praying the psalms is a seemingly
contradictory exercise, whereby we take our entire emotional
landscape to God, and in the very taking, ask God to prune our
landscape and mold it into the shape of the psalms.

The psalms also show something of the character of God. The
God of the psalms is unique ("There is no one like you among
the gods, O Lord, nor are there any works likes yours," Ps. 86:8,

among other passages); God delivers the oppressed (Ps. 103:6, Ps. 146:7); God knows us intimately (Ps. 139; Ps. 56:8); God sustains us (Ps. 40; Ps. 54:4; Ps. 3:5). And just as the Psalter exposes our human emotions, so the psalms also show God feeling and acting alternately delighted, indignant, and enraged.

PAUSE AND CONSIDER In addition to depicting people and God, the psalms also depict nonhuman creatures: trees, animals, oceans, weather. Read psalms 96, 135, and 148. What do these psalms show us about nonhuman creatures?

The psalms make a nice bridge to the New Testament; though many Old Testament books are quoted by New Testament writers, none are quoted as frequently as the Psalter. And the New Testament writers included poetic prayers (or maybe prayerful poems) of their own—such as the song Mary sings when she learns she is pregnant (Luke 1:46–55), the song Simeon sings when he first looks at infant Jesus (Luke 2:29–32), and the hymn of faith Paul includes in his letter to the Philippians (2:6–11). Those texts are psalms of a sort. (And like the Old Testament psalms, many of these New Testament "psalms" have been given central places in Christian liturgy. Episcopalians pray Mary's song, for example, in Morning Prayer and Evening Prayer; and we pray Simeon's song in Morning and Evening Prayer, in Compline, and at funerals.)

More central than the sort-of-psalm to the New Testament is the genre of the **epistle**, or letter. The New Testament includes thirteen letters that tradition has attributed to **Paul**, one of the followers of Jesus who helped spread word of Jesus in the years after his resurrection and ascension, and who helped establish and nurture early church communities from Ephesus to Rome. Modern scholars believe that Paul did not write all thirteen of these letters; some were probably written by early church leaders who were invoking the mantel and authority of Paul. Many of these letters were written to new church communities, churches Paul had helped establish. Paul wanted to continue to give the churches guidance even after he'd left town. The epistles are full of theological riches; they discuss, for example, grace, prayer, and how it might be that one man's death and resurrection has a redemptive impact on the whole cosmos. The epistles also insist that Christian communities practice a certain mode of life—a life that befits members of Jesus's body and conforms to Jesus himself. And, in response to circumstances in the communities to whom the epistles were sent, the epistles often commend specific actions: feed the poor; don't gossip; don't harbor anger. Most readers today can nod along with (even as we basically ignore) "don't gossip." But the epistles also include recommendations that run counter to broadly held assumptions in our contemporary culture. For example, one finds praise of celibacy and encouragement to abstain altogether from marriage and procreation, and one also finds guidelines about gender and sexuality that seem at odds with discernments the Episcopal Church has reached about same-sex marriage and the ordination of women. Reading the epistles is alternately intriguing, maddening, joyful, and painful in part because reading them presses us to ask how the epistles' elemental (and non-negotiable) instruction that Christians live our lives in conformity to Jesus fits together with the specific recommendations Paul and other letter-writers made to particular communities—and what those specific recommendations have to do with our life in Jesus today.

Here are some possible things you might do when you come up against something in the epistles that sounds strange, or that you think is clearly wrong (these, at any rate, are some of the things I do): Sometimes, I shut my Bible and pick up a novel. Sometimes, I begin to research the passage in question; I look for any recent scholarly writing, or patristic or medieval writing, that can help me more fully understand the passage. Sometimes, I look at other passages of the Bible that address the same broad topic—celibacy, marriage, slavery, sex—and think about how those passages might fit together with the epistle passage. And sometimes, I just sit—with my Bible, and with the tension between my sense of what's right and what the Bible seems to say. I'm always curious about what that tension can generate.

Indeed, in terms of genre, I find reading biblical epistles to be one of the most engaging readerly tasks. Paul was writing for specific churches in Corinth and Philippi; he couldn't have envisioned that, two millennia later, I'd be sitting in Durham, North Carolina, reading his missives. Yet, as a Christian, I affirm that in some mysterious but real way, these letters are written for me too, differently but not less than they were written for the early believers in Corinth and Ephesus. That's what makes reading and interpreting the New Testament epistles such a fascinating exercise—reading with the knowledge that the particulars of the letters emerged in response to situations in a given local community, and with the knowledge that the Holy Spirit has something in those particulars somehow for me and my community today.

A few years ago, I found a parcel of letters that my mother wrote to her parents-in-law during her first year of marriage. In the letters, my mother describes, among other things, learning to cook ("When we got married, Linda didn't even know how to boil an egg," my father now says). Mom told Dad's parents about making a soufflé and learning a few different soups. There was one spectacular disaster with marzipan. She also mentions going from Chapel Hill, where she and Dad were living, to Durham, for Chinese food and a movie (*My Fair Lady*). It was strange to read these letters in my own house in Durham, and to think about how I had come to live, years after my mother's death, in this city that had once featured as an anecdote in the letters through which she crafted a tentative friendship with her new husband's parents. My mother, of course, didn't know she was writing these letters to me, too, but I believe I am no less than my grandparents the letters' recipient. I discovered them shortly after divorcing my husband. I was feeling adrift—like I didn't have a family, and like I wasn't equipped to steer my life somewhere sound. Also, my husband had done most of the cooking over the half-decade of our marriage, and I somehow couldn't remember, let alone return to, the casseroles and stews that had been my standbys before I'd met him. I seemed to eat margherita pizzas at a nearby Italian restaurant for dinner most nights.

My mother's letters spoke directly to me. They kept me company, and they helped me sense that perhaps I wasn't as alone as I seemed to be. And they inspired me to begin learning anew how to cook, using some of my mother's old cookbooks. In some curiously time-warped way, I and my twenty-three-year-old mother learned to cook together.

Reading the New Testament epistles is a bit like reading these letters from my mother. The New Testament letters were real letters, written for particular communities, yet they address us today—even though our churches, our questions, and our reading habits are vastly different from the churches, questions, and readings of the first-century Roman Empire.

The New Testament also includes an **apocalypse**, the Revelation of John. (For apocalypse in the Old Testament, look at Daniel 7–11 and at Isaiah 24–27). In our current-day idiom, we tend to say that something is "apocalyptic" if it imagines future destructions: I have "apocalyptic" fantasies of what will happen after another fifty years of climate change. But the word itself simply means "revelation," showing something that has been hidden. The hidden thing revealed in an apocalypse can be a vision of the future. Or an apocalypse can reveal the character of the government under whose rule the apocalyptic author lives, or the character of the people of God. An apocalypse can reveal hidden things that God is doing, and thereby help readers imagine a different, imminent future.

Apocalyptic literature is often written in circumstances of persecution and oppression, and the author is often concerned with charting a way out of present circumstances. The author of Revelation, known to us as John of Patmos, had been exiled to Patmos, a penal colony, where he could expect to work himself to death. There are a lot of confusing and wacky details in Revelation, but at its core, Revelation offers a symbolic picture of how the story of human history will end. It exalts Jesus as king of kings and it proclaims that Jesus will come back and complete the work of healing the world of damage. At the end of Revelation, John of Patmos both confidently affirms that Jesus is coming soon and implores, "Come, Lord Jesus!" Fittingly, Revelation is the last book of the Bible, and when I study it, I like to remind myself that I am, in essence, looking into a crystal ball. I'm being given a stylized and highly literary glimpse of the future—of my future, and of the future of all of creation. How might this future affect my present?

Apocalypses' depictions of the future insist that radical transformation will occur. They stress that the future will be really different from our present. In this way, apocalypses want to show readers what is wrong with the present. That's what I'm doing with my apocalyptic climate change fantasies; these fantasies show me that what I think is most urgently wrong with the present is our treatment of the planet. By contrast, my friend who is rereading Margaret Atwood's *The Handmaid's Tale* for the sixth time thinks that the most urgent problem in the present is the erosion of abortion rights. When I read Revelation, then, I am prompted to ask what problems John of Patmos was diagnosing in his own present, and to ask if they have resonances with today's present.

PAUSE AND CONSIDER One genre that features in both the Old and New Testaments is the **genealogy**—all those lists of "begats." Genealogies are not, as they might appear at first blush, dry records of the generations. Genealogical lists are compressed stories, and those who write the lists tend to include some people and leave other people out. Through selective inclusion and exclusion, the writer of the genealogy is trying to focus the reader's attention on the relationships the writer thinks is most important (and sometimes, the writer omits, and thus tries to divert attention away from, branches of the family tree he or she is embarrassed by).

One of the most striking biblical genealogies is Matthew 1:1–16, which traces Jesus's lineage all the way back to Abraham. The genealogy mentions four women from the Old Testament. This is odd; lineage was typically traced only through men. Read the genealogy in Matthew. Then read the stories of the four Old Testament women mentioned there: Tamar's story is found in Genesis 38; Rahab's in Joshua 2 and Joshua 6; Ruth in the Book of Ruth (it's one of two biblical books to be named after a woman); and Bathsheba's in 2 Samuel 11–12. What do you notice about these women? What might Matthew have been trying to do in highlighting their place in the lineage of Jesus? Matthew also mentions Mary, the mother of Jesus. (Luke 1–2 is one of the places in the New Testament where you can read about her.) Does Mary have anything in common with the other women mentioned? Why do you think this genealogy was so important to Matthew that he began his Gospel with it?

We'll conclude our look at biblical genre by considering the four books that, for many Christian readers, constitute the center of the Bible: the four **Gospels**.

When we read from the Gospels in church on Sunday, the deacon or priest introduces the reading by saying "The Gospel of our Lord Jesus Christ according to Matthew" or "The Gospel of our Lord Jesus Christ according to Mark." That introductory phrasing encapsulates, in its three parts, what a Gospel is.

- First, we call these texts "Gospels," a word that means "good tidings" or "good announcement."

- Second, we name these good tidings as, specifically, the good tidings of our Lord Jesus.

- Third, we recognize four Gospels, written by four different authors: Matthew, Mark, Luke, and John. Each author wrote for a different audience, and each wrote with different interests; thus, though each Gospel is fundamentally interested in *recounting* and *interpreting* the life of Jesus, each Gospel puts a slightly different spin on things. The Gospel of Luke, for example, is especially interested in Jesus as one who paid attention to women, the poor, and other marginalized people. Thus, Luke begins his account of Jesus's adult ministry by depicting Jesus quoting the prophet Isaiah's declaration that "the Spirit of the Lord is upon me, because he has anointed me to bring good news to the poor. He has sent me to proclaim release to the captives and recovery of sight to the blind, to let the oppressed go free, to proclaim the year of the Lord's favor" (Luke 4:18–19). The Gospel of Matthew, by contrast, is especially interested in showing that Jesus is the *Jewish* messiah; thus, Matthew pays a lot of attention to Jesus's family lineage; Matthew presents Jesus as having come to save the "lost sheep of Israel"; and so forth.

Thus, what we read in the Gospels are four versions of the good tidings—the Good News—that Christians believe we find in, about, and through Jesus Christ.

For many years, I thought the Gospels were, essentially, short biographies—accounts of the life of Jesus of Nazareth. But increasingly, I've realized that this is an inadequate encapsulation of what the Gospels are, for two reasons.

First, if they're biographies, they're not very good biographies, since, aside from a few details about Jesus's birth and infancy, and one snapshot of his boyhood, the Gospels are focused almost entirely on the events immediately preceding and following his death. In other words, there's a great deal about Jesus's life that is left out of the Gospels; in terms of comprehensiveness, calling them biographies would be like calling an account of Abraham Lincoln's years in the White House his biography.

Second, the Gospels aim not just to recount events from Jesus's life, but to show us that his teachings, and his life, death, and resurrection, are quintessential good tidings. The Gospels show us that the shape of Jesus's life enacts what Jesus says. When I receive the Gospels not as biographies but as Gospels—as the good tidings of the One who is what he says—I can ask some questions not just of the text, but of my own life. Does the shape of my life enact what I say? Or, more important, does it enact what Jesus says?

Chapter 4

The Liturgy
of the Word

I intensely dislike reading microfilm, but there I was, at the Library of Virginia in Richmond, working my way through a reel unpromisingly called "Virginia Miscellany, miscellaneous reel 19." These were documents from the eighteenth century, and I was searching for morsels for my doctoral dissertation, which considered the ways Anglicans in colonial Virginia practiced their Christian faith at home—around the dinner table, in private prayer, in the production of needlework that depicted biblical scenes, and so forth. (This is not a good topic to pick if you hate microfilm.)

Reel 19 included a few intriguing hints about Anglicans in Virginia. There was a screed by one unnamed Anglican criticizing the Presbyterians. There was a document that spelled out what pains a "beneficed Clergyman" (that is, a priest with a permanent, paying job) would suffer if he spoke "any thing in the

Derogation, or depraving of the Book of Common Prayer." And there was a letter written by a clergyman who had raised money to buy Bibles, prayer books, and other religious tomes, to be given to "the Poor of this Parish." It was important, even urgent, the clergyman argued, that baptized Christians have access to books that would help them understand the "Nature of the solemn Vow that they made" in baptism; men with money should make sure their "Servants & poor Neighbours be supplied with such good Books."

In the middle of this letter was a sentence that seemed to me as applicable to the present as it was to the eighteenth century. "[I]t is a peculiar Advantage of the Members of the Church of England," wrote the clergyman, "that if they frequent the publick prayers, they constantly hear a considerable Portion of the Holy Scriptures read to them." People still needed Bibles at home, this clergyman thought, but if they didn't have them—well, at least they'd hear a lot of Scripture at church on Sunday.

It is still a "peculiar Advantage" that Episcopalians hear a hefty dose of Scripture in church on Sunday worship. In fact, in a given Sunday service, Episcopalians typically hear more Scripture, and we typically hear from more books of the Bible, than do worshippers in many other Christian communities. And for most Episcopalians, the encounter with Scripture on Sunday morning is our most consistent, sustained engagement with Scripture all week.

The Scriptures feature in two central ways in a Eucharist service. In this chapter, we'll consider the reading of Scripture in the section of the service known as the Liturgy of the Word (the Word in question is the Bible). In the next chapter, we'll look at some of the words from Scripture that thread unannounced all through the liturgy.

Proclaimed in the Liturgy of the Word

> The reading of Scripture in the church is a part of
> our church liturgy, a special portion of the service
> we do to God.
> —*Richard Hooker*

The first half of a Eucharist service focuses on proclaiming, listening to, and responding to Scripture. What passages of Scripture do we read on a given Sunday? The passages aren't selected by the priest or by the church worship committee. Rather, the readings follow a table of appointed readings called a **lectionary** (the word comes from the Latin word *lectio*, to read; a lectionary is a list of the Scripture passages *to be read* aloud in church). Sometimes the lectionary gives an option—read this Old Testament passage or that Old Testament passage—but generally, because Episcopalians follow the lectionary, every Episcopal church in the country reads the same Scripture passages on a given Sunday. For the last forty-five years or so, many other churches have followed the same lectionary (it's called the **Revised Common Lectionary**), so it's entirely possible that your neighbors who attend a Methodist or Lutheran or Roman Catholic church have heard the same Scripture passages.

Beyond ensuring that Christians in many different communities hear the same Scriptures on a given Sunday, the lectionary has many benefits. Chiefly, it prevents your priest from simply selecting her favorite biblical passages to read and preach over and over. As a preacher, I find living inside the contours of the lectionary a challenging and wonderful gift. The lectionary invites me to attend—in my preaching, study, and prayer—to biblical texts I might otherwise skip, because I find them frustrating or bewildering or dull.

But there are some drawbacks to the lectionary—and, as is usually true in life, the drawbacks are the inverse of the benefits. Yes, the lectionary guarantees my congregation isn't subjected to my favorite biblical texts all the time. Yet, when my Presbyterian pastor friend, who doesn't follow the lectionary, tells me he is preaching through Paul's letter to Romans for four months, I envy his congregation's experience of immersing deeply in one biblical book week after week. A second drawback of the lectionary is the range of Old Testament texts read. If left to their own devices, many pastors would gravitate toward New Testament texts; the lectionary corrects for that, and guarantees that a healthy dose of Old Testament passages is read in church. And yet, the lectionary ultimately includes only a tiny percentage of Old Testament readings, and it tends to pair the Old Testament readings with New Testament readings in a way that suggests a particular interpretation—rather than letting the Old Testament readings stand as their own proclamation of the word of God and God's activity in the world, the lectionary pushes us to hear the Old Testament as a being "fulfilled" by events that happen in the New Testament.

It is worth pausing here to clarify just what the terms **"Old Testament"** and **"New Testament"** mean. In the third century, Christians began referring to the Jewish scriptures that they had adopted into Christian life and worship as *palaia diatheke* (Greek) or *vetus testamentum* (Latin), and the writings about the life and death of Jesus of Nazareth and the early church as the *kaine diatheke* or *novum testamentum*. The English renderings of those phrases—"Old Testament" and "New Testament"—were in use by the fourteenth century. Today, many people find "Old Testament" and "New Testament" problematic, because they can be (and often have been) taken to imply that the stuff of the Old Testament—God's work, before the birth of Jesus of Nazareth, with the Jewish people—is outdated, outmoded, and has been superseded and replaced by the "new" work that God is doing in and through Jesus and the church. Because of this implication, some Christians choose to refer to the two testaments as the First and Second Testaments, or the Hebrew Bible and the Christian Bible. In this book, and in my speech and writing generally, I retain, with some ambivalence, "Old Testament" and "New Testament." I take seriously the concerns that have led many to reject those terms, but I retain them principally to make clear that when I read and pray and speak about these texts, I am doing so *as a Christian*, not as a disinterested academic student, or as a practicing Jew. As a Christian, I affirm that both testaments are equally the Christian Bible, and I explicitly reject the notion that the Old Testament is outmoded and has been replaced by the New Testament. Indeed, "old" need not carry the connotation "outmoded." When I look around my house, I see that practically everything I like is "old," and derives meaning in part from layered associations lent by age: the pink dessert plates that were my great-grandmother's; the abolitionist embroidery, declaring in bold stitches "How Sweet is Liberty"; the KitchenAid mixer my mother was given in 1969, which somehow still works. Honestly, I find all these old things more interesting than their newer counterparts, and the cake plates' and embroidery's distinctive flavor are in my mind when I refer to the "Old Testament." (And at least one verse in the Bible agrees with me—Luke 5:39: "no one after drinking old wine desires new wine, but says, 'The old is good.'")

PAUSE AND CONSIDER People have strong opinions about the use of the terms "Old Testament" and "New Testament." What do you think and why?

Now, then, following the lectionary, Episcopalians typically read four passages of Scripture, usually two Old Testament readings and two New Testament readings. The normal pattern is:

A reading from the Old Testament,* but not a psalm, followed by

a psalm, followed by

a reading from any New Testament book other than the Gospels or the Acts of the Apostles, followed by

a reading from a Gospel, followed by

a sermon.

Notice the second reading, a psalm. The psalms, remember, are prayers, and for most of church history, they have been the bedrock of Christian corporate worship. In other Episcopal services, like Morning and Evening Prayer, they're even more central (arguably, Morning and Evening Prayer simply are recitations of psalms, decorated with a bit of additional Scripture and prayer), but even in our Eucharistic liturgy, we do things that set the psalm apart from the other readings. The psalm is not concluded by an exchange like "The Word of the Lord," "Thanks be to God." It is often read in unison by the entire congregation, or sung by a choir. Sometimes, we read or sing a verse called an **antiphon** (the word comes from the Greek for "responsive sound") before and after the psalm—the antiphon may itself be drawn from the Psalter, and it often connects the psalm to the liturgical season (Advent, Lent, etc). The psalm, then, is at once a constitutive part of the set of four readings, and it's different from the other three.

---

* During the fifty-day season of Easter, the Old Testament reading is replaced with a reading from the Acts of the Apostles. Acts shows us the earliest Christians, after Jesus's resurrection and ascension, figuring out how to live as a community that worships the risen Christ; Eastertide is an appropriate time to hear Acts.

All of these markings indicate that the congregation is *praying* the psalm in a way that we're not fully praying the other readings.

Notice, also, the order of the readings. If you flip to the table of contents in your Bible, you'll see that we read the Scriptures in church in a different order than the order given in your table of contents. Most obviously, in church services, we read the Gospel last—that is, after we've read New Testament texts that occur later in the table of contents, such as passages from Acts or the epistles. The order in your table of contents is known as the "canonical order" of Scripture. The canonical order developed gradually and had been fixed by the late fourth century. At a Eucharist, we follow a different order—one that crowns the Gospel as the summit of all our biblical reading.

Placing the Gospels last in our church reading is just one way we set these passages apart. We introduce and conclude the Gospel reading with slightly different words than the formulations we use to introduce and conclude the other Scripture readings: to introduce the other readings, people might simply say "the first reading is from Isaiah," and they conclude the reading by naming it "the word of the Lord"; when we read the Gospel, we say "the Gospel of our Lord Jesus Christ according to John," and at the conclusion, we name the reading as "The Gospel of the Lord," not "the Word of the Lord." Similarly, the congregation acclaims "Thanks be to God" after all the other readings, but before and after the Gospel, the congregation says "Glory to you, Lord Christ," and "Praise to you, Lord Christ." We stand for the reading of the Gospel. The Gospel is read by a clergyperson, while typically the other readings are read by a layperson. We read the Gospel passage from a special book, and we sometimes process with that book into the center of the congregation; in some churches, the Gospel book is bathed in incense before the Gospel passage is read.

It's significant that we read four passages from different parts of Scripture. That we do so testifies to our belief that we meet and hear from God in all biblical books. The multiplicity of readings also honors Scripture as a collection of texts that encompasses many different voices and many different perspectives.

And yet, even as we read from the entire corpus of Scripture in worship, our Gospel procession and the order in which we read biblical passages mark the Gospel as privileged within the whole Scripture reading. I admit this makes me uncomfortable. I worry about the implicit message this sends—that God is somehow most available in the Gospels, and that the Old Testament, in particular, isn't as wholly God's abundant word as are the Gospels.

Yet, alongside that worry, I can appreciate the liturgical ordering of Scripture readings. Why, in the Eucharist service, does the Gospel stand apart as the pinnacle of Scripture? Perhaps for two reasons. First, the larger choreography of the service points to Jesus's becoming present to us in the Eucharist, which follows the Liturgy of the Word; by ordering the Scripture readings to culminate in a Gospel passage about the life of Jesus, the momentum of the Scripture readings builds toward Jesus, and thus directs worshippers to Jesus-in-the-Eucharist. Second, the Gospels contain the words of Jesus; Isaiah and Paul's letter to the Romans do not. So the Gospels bring us the words of God in a double sense—as Christians, we believe that all Scripture is the word of God, but the words spoken by the incarnate God and then recorded in the Gospels are the words of God in a concentrated, intensified way.

Finally, notice the **sermon**. There's little agreement among Christians about exactly what a sermon is and what it should aim to do. But I'll hazard this: by definition, a sermon is a discursive response to at least one of the Scripture passages just proclaimed. If the person in the pulpit is not engaging with and responding to the Scriptures, she's not preaching a sermon.

The sermon aims to interpret the Scripture that has just been proclaimed, and to do so in a way that speaks directly to the congregation, interlacing Scripture with the people in church and their situation in the world. Preaching, then, is a way of extending the intimate reach of the Scriptures; it's a way of allowing the Scriptures to become part of a congregation's local particularities.

Sermons also exhort people to do something in response to the Scriptures—to love, to give, to think differently about something than they had thought an hour ago, to turn their gaze from anxiety or anger to Jesus, indeed to seek out Jesus when they leave church. In addressing the circumstances of the congregation and in exhorting the congregation to respond to the Scriptures, the sermon tries to help the entire congregation see how Scripture grips us.

> "The people (by . . . hearyng . . . holy scripture read in the Churche) should continuallye profite more and more in the knowledge of God, and bee the more inflamed with the love of his true religion."
> —*Thomas Cranmer, Preface of the 1549 edition of the Book of Common Prayer*

Your Body, Listening to Scripture in Worship

What do you actually do with your body in church when the Scripture is being read?

Some people attend to the Scriptures with their eyes, reading along, either with a Bible, or, more typically in an Episcopal church, with a worship bulletin that includes the day's appointed Scriptures.

Other people listen, attending to the Scripture readings with their ears. I am hard of hearing, so it's easier for me to read along—I miss some of the words when I only listen. But nonetheless, that's what I try to do—to put my worship bulletin down and listen to the reading from Exodus or the reading from 1 Corinthians. If it were up to me, this would be the standard practice in Episcopal churches—and not only because so doing would connect us to other Christians, since for most of church history (and still in many parts of the world today), Christians in corporate worship experienced the Scriptures by hearing it, not by reading the words on a page. I'd prefer we listen exactly because, for most twenty-first-century Americans, listening to something being read to us is an unusual experience. Other than church, my primary experience of being read to dates to childhood—being read books by my parents and teachers. When I listen in church as I listened in childhood, I am immediately placed in a position of receptivity that I don't typically occupy.

> "When you see a group of baptized people listening to the Bible in public worship, you realize that Bible-reading is an essential part of Christian life because *Christian life is a listening life*. Christians are people who expect to be spoken to by God."
> —*Rowan Williams*

A medieval church tradition imagined that Mary conceived through her ear. As Agobard of Lyon puts it in one representative aural account of the Annunciation, "He, light and God of the created universe, descends from heaven, sent forth from the breast of the Father; having put on the purple stole, he enters our region through the ear of the Virgin." *Conceptio per aurem* ("conception through the ear") is more than just a quaint medievalism (which served the medieval church in part because it provided a way to think about Mary conceiving a child yet remaining a virgin; she was impregnated through a different bodily orifice). To "conceive" means "to become pregnant with a child," and it also means "to form an intention in the mind or heart" ("Why hast thou conceived this thing in thine heart?" Peter asks the duplicitous Ananias in Acts 5:4, KJV). Mary conceived a child through her ear, said the medievals; when I listen to the Scriptures in church, I might find the sounded word plants an intention in my heart. I am, in a very small way, imitating Mary, trying to find an openness to whatever God wants to root and gestate in me.

PAUSE AND CONSIDER Recall a moment when you felt especially connected with the Bible. What helps you to pay attention to (or even "digest") Scripture? Reading it or hearing it? Encountering Scripture in community or on your own? In church or somewhere else entirely?

There is, to be sure, an art to listening to Scripture in church. All of us—including priests—sometimes struggle to pay attention to the Scripture readings. I am trying to develop the practice of sitting quietly in the church sanctuary before the service starts, and mulling over what's going on in my life and in the world. I ask God to direct my attention to knots, to things I'm confused and unsettled about. And then I ask God to help me to hear something about these knots in the worship service. I don't manage to do this every Sunday, but when I do, it helps me listen for a word from God during the readings of the Scriptures. Because I've reminded myself about those situations about which I most deeply need a word, I become more able to hear that word when it shows up.

Chapter 5

Praying the Scriptures

The historian of liturgy Hughes Oliphant Old once observed that "prayer, particularly Christian prayer, uses biblical language. . . . The Bible contains a vast number of paradigms for prayer and a thesaurus of words to handle the unique experience of prayer." The Book of Common Prayer is a paradigmatic instance of the use of biblical language in prayer. If you are familiar with the church's Sunday prayers, you know more Bible than you realize.

Indeed, at a Sunday Eucharist, words of Scripture are almost the first words we say. After an opening hymn, the priest and the congregation exchange a greeting. During the season of Lent, that greeting is

> Bless the Lord who forgives all our sins. * *His mercy endures for ever.*

During the season of Easter, it's

> Alleluia. Christ is risen. * *The Lord is risen indeed. Alleluia.*

During the rest of the year, the greeting is

> Blessed be God: Father, Son, and Holy Spirit. * *And blessed be his kingdom, now and for ever. Amen.*

Each of those formulations has its roots in Scripture. "Blessed be God" is a phrase proclaimed in several places in the Old Testament; when I open the service with those words, I like to think they are especially attached to the psalmist's use of them in Psalm 66. There the psalmist says, "Blessed be God, because he has not rejected my prayer or removed his steadfast love from me" (v. 20). This feels like a wonderful note on which to start our service—an affirmation and a reminder, as we begin to pray, that God does not reject our prayers. The penitential words with which we begin the service during Lent are also drawn from the psalms; they echo Psalm 103:2–3 ("Bless the Lord, O my soul . . . who forgives all your iniquity"). Finally, during the Easter season, we quote the Gospel of Luke's account of what the disciples said on the first Easter, as they were beginning to make sense of the rumors that Jesus was alive: "The Lord has risen indeed," they said to one another.

After this opening acclamation, we say the collect for purity, which echoes Psalm 51. Then, in many of our churches, we sing or recite the prayer known as "the Gloria," a prayer of praise that dates to the fourth century. Its first line—"glory to God in the highest, and peace to his people on earth"—is drawn from the Christmas story, from the second chapter of the Gospel of Luke. Right after Mary gives birth, an angel appears to a group of shepherds. The angel proclaims that the messiah has been born, and tells the shepherds they'll know they've found the messiah when they come upon "a child wrapped in bands of cloth and lying in a manger." And then, suddenly, a large batch of additional angels appears, and all those angels together proclaim the words we say on Sunday mornings:

Glory to God in the highest, and peace to his people on earth.

It is, perhaps, the hearing of those holy words that allowed the shepherds to recognize God in the form of an unregistered, undocumented newborn in a barn, and reciting them on Sundays may help us recognize Jesus in one another and in the bread and wine.

Before we get to the official reading of the Bible, we've already been saturated in the words of Scripture.

Similarly, the section of the Eucharist that follows the Scripture readings is stitched together from biblical phrases. We begin turning our attention fully to the Eucharist when the bread and wine are brought forward to the altar or table (donations of money might also be collected and brought forward). Just before the bread and wine are brought forward, the priest says a sentence taken from Scripture—the sentence might be "Walk in love, as Christ loved us and gave himself for us, an offering and sacrifice to God" (from Paul's letter to the Ephesians); or it might be "Worship the Lord in the beauty of holiness" (from Psalm 96) or some other biblical verse that encapsulates something of what is happening in the Eucharist.

And then we enter the long prayers over the bread and wine. The arc of these prayers is scriptural, echoing and retelling the Bible's account of the Last Supper (found in Matthew 26, Mark 14, Luke 22, and 1 Corinthians 11). They also include the congregation's praying the **Lord's Prayer**, which is first given to Jesus's followers by Jesus, as recorded in Matthew 6 and Luke 11. The major pieces of the Eucharistic liturgies, then, are either

direct quotations from the Bible (as in the Lord's Prayer) or para-
phrases of biblical texts.

So much of what we say when we gather together on Sunday morning is drawn from the Bible that it might be accurate
to say *Christian communal worship is people getting together
and returning to God the words that God has given us in the
Bible.* For Episcopalians (and for some other members of the
larger Christian family, like Roman Catholics), Scripture is not
one element among many in communal worship; Scripture is the
fundamental element of worship.

Why does so much of our communal worship comprise the
recitation of Scripture? The biblical book 1 Chronicles depicts
the people of Israel bringing gold, silver, and precious stones to
be used in the building of the temple. King David surveys these
offerings, and says to God: "For all things come from you, and
of your own have we given you. . . . O LORD our God, all this
abundance that we have provided for building you a house for
your holy name comes from your hand and is all your own" (1
Chronicles 29:14, 16).

"All things come of Thee, O Lord, and of thine own have
we given thee." In earlier editions of the prayer book (madden-
ingly lost from our current edition), that sentence is included in
the list of biblical sentences that a priest might say just before
the bread and wine are brought to the table. The prayer book
included that sentence because it recognized that at the Eucharist, we offer to God something that God first gave us. We
didn't create the wheat or the grapes; God made them, and now
we give to God bread and wine that we made from the stores
God gave us.

The centrality of biblical words and biblical phrases in worship is just like bread and wine; when we stitch our prayers

together from biblical phrases, we are offering God's own words back to God, and we're acknowledging, in a sense, that no words we could offer God are fully ours—they're always words we've received first from God, and, just as we make wine from grapes, we've managed to make some prayers with words God authored.

The Bible itself shows us that one good thing to do with the words of the Bible is offer them back to God in prayer. For example, in the first chapter of the Gospel of Luke, Mary offers a stunning prayer, praising God for the strange thing God has done in making her pregnant with the Messiah. Mary is not making this prayer up out of whole cloth. She draws on a prayer she would have known from 1 Samuel, a prayer of thanksgiving Hannah prayed after she became pregnant. Even Jesus did not concoct all his prayers from whole cloth. As he was being put to death, Jesus himself offered the words of Psalm 22 to God the Father.

PAUSE AND CONSIDER Read the story of Mary's pregnancy (Luke 1:26–55). Then read the story of Hannah's pregnancy (1 Samuel 1:1–2:10). What does Mary seem to be doing with the text of Hannah's prayer? Then flip back even further, to Exodus 15:19–21, where you'll find the prayer known as the song of Miriam. This song is older than Hannah's prayer. How are Hannah and Mary using the words or ideas of Exodus 15 in their prayers?

To be sure, there are plenty of words in our communal prayers that don't come directly from Scripture. Some of the words were written by Christians in the third century or the sixteenth century or the twentieth century. Those extrabiblical words are, to use a culinary metaphor, binding agents: they are like tapioca in a blueberry pie. The blueberries are the point of the pie, but the tapioca thickens the berries and holds them together.

Sometimes it strikes me as odd that so much of our communal worship consists of reciting words of Scripture back to God. It strikes me as odd, I think, because simply reciting God's words back to God doesn't seem to leave much room for my personal, individual prayers.

Of course, a life of prayer does include each of us simply talking to God—about our feelings, about our questions. I tend to do that kind of praying while I'm walking to work, or when I can't sleep at night. Even there, however, I find I don't always have very good words for my own deep emotions; when I'm angry, I often find that praying Psalm 109 is as direct a way of taking that anger to God as venting the specifics of my fury at my sister, who yet again managed to elide my whole adulthood in a single phrase.

I am increasingly trying to allow the liturgy's reliance on scriptural language to shape my understanding of what Scripture and prayer are. If the church's worship consists largely of reciting Scripture, then Scripture in part is the text Christians pray together. And if the church's worship consists largely of reciting Scripture, then prayer isn't foremost about carrying my individual concerns to God. Prayer, rather, is about offering to God something—some sentences, some odes—we've made from words God first gave us.

> "Very much of our liturgy is the very words of Scripture."
> —*Jeremy Taylor*

There's no perfect analogy here, but perhaps speaking to God from God's own store of scriptural words is a bit like the beloved who, upon hearing her lover declare "I love you," says "I love you too." She doesn't feel compelled to come up with an original response; she simply wants to return the ardor.

Or perhaps speaking to God from God's own store of scriptural words is a bit like the kind of conversation you have when you get together with your siblings, whom you only see twice a year. You always tell the same anecdotes, and you slip into old family idioms you never use with anyone else—but when you're with your sisters, those turns-of-phrase seem so natural that you barely notice what you're saying. This exchange of family clichés is comfortable and a little boring; the clichés knit you together, and they need to be said.

Or perhaps speaking to God from God's own store of scriptural words is a bit like actors performing a play in front of the playwright.

My favorite playwright is Sarah Ruhl. In a 2007 interview, Ruhl talked about watching a recent production of her play *The Clean House*:

> It was exactly the play and yet more so, because there were elements I would never have thought of that were so sublime. For instance, there's a scene where Lane, a doctor married to a doctor, imagines her husband kissing the breast of his new lover, who is one of his patients. The stage direction says, "Ana wears a gown. Is it a hospital gown or a ballroom gown?" Well, Marilyn Dodds Frank, who plays Ana, walked out in a renaissance ball gown made of lavender hospital-gown material. It had a train that was about 20 yards long. So she begins walking out in this purple gown, and it just keeps coming and coming and coming. I would never have thought of that. That was a high point of my life really, watching that production and thinking: They really read my mind.

I wonder if God ever experiences our worship that way— like we've taken the script of Scripture and thrown in an insane lavender gown that God didn't think of, and in so doing, we've somehow gotten to the essence of the script, and delighted the playwright.

Elsewhere in the same interview, Ruhl says that although she's always pleased and impressed by the productions of her plays, she'd "like to discover what would happen if I worked with the same actors and designers over and over in a concentrated way. If the actor and I were able to know exactly what we meant if I said, 'Give this line a little more space.' As opposed to one actor who thinks space is a subtext and another who thinks space is a technical pause." This seems like a good way to think about what we do as a church community, week in and week out. I doubt I'll ever know "exactly" what God means when God asks us to give a line a bit more space. But it's nice to imagine that years from now, after many more years of working together on the scripts that are our Scripture-saturated prayers, I and my church community might be able to more natively inhabit the script.

One more insight, culled from the theater, about why so much of our worship consists in returning words of the Bible to God: A book I recently read by voice coach Catherine Weate observes that when we're around people we're intimate with, we often unconsciously "shadow each other's words and rhythms." Indeed, among those we love, we sometimes lapse into what's called "allo-repetition," repeating back to someone what she has said first. We might, for example, use a word our friend has just used, or we might repeat her entire sentence with tiny modifications of diction or punctuation (when your friend says "Do you want to know what happened to me today?" you don't reply "yes"; you reply "I *do* want to know what happened to you today!"). When we allo-repeat, we are showing that we're paying attention to our friend; we're affirming that what she's said is important;

and, ultimately, by borrowing her speech, we strengthen and cement our bond to her. Our habit of borrowing God's words when speaking to God is not, therefore, a sign that our real selves are somehow not engaged in prayer; to the contrary, our use of Scripture in worship is precisely a sign, and an agent, of our intimacy with God.

Chapter 6

Life, Death, and Everything in Between

The Sunday service of Holy Eucharist is one space in which a worshipper at an Episcopal church will encounter Scripture, but, of course, Sunday morning Eucharist is not the only service that sometimes draws people to church. If you thumb through the Book of Common Prayer, you'll notice how much Scripture shapes other liturgies.

- The service of **Morning Prayer** (which can be prayed on a weekday, or on a Sunday in lieu of a Eucharist) begins with an opening sentence of Scripture, and then organizes itself centrally around praying psalms and reciting other Scripture passages.

- The **Easter Vigil**, which is celebrated the Saturday night before Easter Sunday, includes a staggering eleven Bible readings—plus psalms.

- The late-night prayer service **Compline** (the name comes from the Latin word *completa*, complete or filled full) consists almost entirely in praying psalms and other biblical passages.

All of these services—Eucharist, Morning Prayer, Compline, the Easter Vigil—are services whose orientation toward God is obvious, even blunt: worshipping God is the straightforward, self-evident purpose of those services (although they have many other effects, such as providing an occasion for us to mingle with friends). Scripture features significantly in those worship services exactly because the best words to speak to God are those words God has spoken first to us.

Scripture also features in the services whose central aims more clearly include not just connecting people with God, but also nurturing our relationships with other human beings: weddings and funerals. Weddings and funerals mark major passages in people's lives. And that is why we read the Bible at them—because we need to hear God talking to us about dying, and about getting married. We want to understand what death and marriage, family and bereavement, and partnership and commitment and loss mean—and the church invites us to read Scripture at the events that celebrate those losses and commitments because we can understand what they mean only in the context of pondering what God says about them. So we read Scripture at these life events with the same expectation that we always bring to Scripture: the expectation that we will hear God speak to us.

The prayer book makes some suggestions about which Scripture passages might be read at the service—the wedding suggestions are on page 426 of the prayer book, and the funeral passages on 494 and 495—but neither the prayer book, nor any lectionary, dictates the final selection. (So there you are in the shock of grief, and not having been to church much in the last few years, and you're not even sure you own a Bible—and suddenly a priest is asking you which Bible passages you want read at Mother's funeral.) How might one select Bible passages for a wedding or funeral? And what might one listen for when one attends a wedding or funeral in an Episcopal church?

Scripture at Weddings

Of the biblical passages the prayer book suggests for weddings, my favorite is the passage from the Song of Solomon 2:10–13. It begins:

My beloved speaks and says to me:
"Arise, my love, my fair one,
and come away;
for now the winter is past,
the rain is over and gone.
The flowers appear on the earth;
the time of singing has come,
and the voice of the turtledove
is heard in our land.
The fig tree puts forth its figs,
and the vines are in blossom;
they give forth fragrance.
Arise, my love, my fair one,
and come away."

This passage captures the frank emotion of a wedding. The speaker is talking about something he really wants and doesn't yet have: the promise of love and intimacy. There's a sense in the text that the speaker believes he has good reason to think he's going to get these things, and he is eager to get to it. The passage is about sex, but it's also about our longing to be enfolded into the embrace of another person, to be loved and desired. The speaker is ready for all that to be consummated, and even the natural world is ready: the figs want to be eaten, the flowers want to be smelled, and the couple is ready to be together; we were once in the wintry wasteland of not having one another, but now we have each other, and we are saying to each other "arise, and come away with me."

If I had my druthers, this passage would be read at every single wedding, because it evokes the excitement and urgency that the marrying couple (presumably) feels.

And then, in what strikes me as a brilliant bit of ellipsis, the prayer book pairs those vine-blossoming, anticipatory verses of the Song of Solomon with a few verses from a later chapter of the same book:

> Set me as a seal upon your heart,
> as a seal upon your arm;
> for love is strong as death,
> passion fierce as the grave.
> Its flashes are flashes of fire,
> a raging flame.
> Many waters cannot quench love,
> neither can floods drown it.
> If one offered for love
> all the wealth of one's house,
> it would be utterly scorned.
> (Song of Solomon 8:6–7)

The first bit of the Song is about anticipation; the second section is about durability. The seal language recognizes that the urgent hunger isn't durable. The couple needs to be set in one another as a clay or wax seal is set, and it's the wedding—the vows, the blessing, the confecting ritual—that does the setting.

Taken as whole, then, the Song of Solomon passage addresses two weddings keystones: desire and endurance. Those themes are about the feelings and needs of the couple, and by itself, the Song of Solomon passage has little to say about anyone other than the nuptial couple. Yet, the wedding is attended by other people, and the wedding is also a service in which participants worship God. The other Scripture passages you're likely to hear at an Episcopal wedding point beyond the marrying couple, suggesting that marriage isn't only or even principally about the couple. Rather, marriage relates the couple to their larger community and to Jesus in a particular way.

Many of the suggested wedding passages have nothing specifically to do with marriage, eros, or romance. Except for the Song of Solomon text, the passages that discuss "love"—love is patient, love is kind (1 Corinthians 13:1–13); let us love one another for love is of God (1 John 4:7–16)—are about a broader, more diffuse love: the love of Christian community. Consider, for example, the suggested passage from the Gospel of John:

> As the Father has loved me, so I have loved you; abide in my love. If you keep my commandments, you will abide in my love, just as I have kept my Father's commandments and abide in his love. I have said these things to you so that my joy may be in you, and that your joy may be complete. "This is my commandment, that you love one another as I have loved you." (15:9–12)

This comes from the long speech Jesus gives his closest friends during the Last Supper, shortly before he is put to death by the Roman government. When we read it at a wedding, we are suggesting that marital love is a species or a subset of the love of the larger Christian community—and that suggestion is both true and untrue. In one sense, the very reason Christians don't, normatively, elope is that Christians believe that even our seemingly private romantic arrangements aren't private. Insofar as we are part of the body of Christ, our fundamental commitments—even our *intimate* fundamental commitments—are part of the body of Christ too; our romance is subsidiary to the church. And yet, even as we always say at Christian weddings that the gathered community of friends and relatives is there pledging to uphold the couple in their vows, there is a sense in which nuptial love does create a small, intense community of two; for the most part, married people have to work out their marriage alone. For good and for ill, the community is not crawling in bed with you at night.

The Song of Solomon passage pairs nicely with the suggested passage from 1 John, which wrenches our attention from erotic longing *a deux* to God. The author of 1 John 4 shows that loving God is necessarily implicated with loving other people, and vice versa: if you can't love God, 1 John seems to say, you can't love other people; and if you don't love your neighbor whom you have seen, how can you love God, whom you haven't seen? If you love any other person, you know God because the act of your loving makes you a participant in the God who is Love. This is a wonderful passage to read at a wedding because everyone in the congregation, married or not, can locate themselves and whatever loves pepper their lives inside the love of God. But the passage also specifically addresses the marrying couple, suggesting to them that in loving one another as fully as they do, they are participating as completely as human beings can in the God who made them—the God who made them with love and the God who made them to be lovers.

The passage from 1 John shows us that when we love another person, we are reaching beyond ourselves—to the person we love, yes, but also even further: our love of another person relates us somehow both to other people *and to God*. This passage deepens what we think we know about weddings. We know, already, that love takes us beyond our self to another person— that's why people get married. The 1 John passage extends that knowledge, reminding us that God brought us into being out of nothing by loving us before we even existed—*we are, because we were loved*. That, of course, is what each partner in the marriage is doing for the other: they are repeating God's own action, making the other exist as a beloved-other, which is one of the few things you cannot do for yourself.

PAUSE AND CONSIDER Many biblical texts use weddings, brides, and bridegrooms as metaphors for the church's relationship to God. For example, in Revelation 19:7–9, wedding imagery evokes the future that God is planning for us. Currently, the Revelation text implies, we are being courted by God, or perhaps we are engaged to God (one sixth-century commentary on Revelation delightfully adds that the church has received the Holy Spirit as a courtship gift from God—maybe as an engagement ring). At the end of time, we will come to a "marriage supper," at which God will marry God's beloved people. What would your spiritual life be like if you understood yourself to be engaged to God? Why have these nuptial metaphors been so enduring in the church?

Scripture at Funerals

The biblical passages typically read at Episcopal funerals speak directly to the reality of death. Indeed, the passages take up a double task—they acknowledge the sorrow of the mourner and offer her some comfort, and they anticipate the resurrection of the dead.

The *locus classicus* of that double task is the passage from Job. Job has been utterly undone by loss—he has lost all of his animals; he's lost his money; he's lost his children. As the passage opens, Job laments to his friends that the hand of the Lord has smitten him; he foresees his own rotting corpse. And yet even so, Job can declare, "I know that my Redeemer lives," and he is confident he'll see God. In this same passage, Job says, "O that my words were written down! O that they were inscribed in a book!" (19:23). Of course, we can read those words because they were, in fact, inscribed in a book. At first blush, this discussion of writing doesn't seem related to the work of a funeral, but I think it is deeply related. Job's words, finally, are written down in the heart of God; they are heard by God, tended by God, and remembered by God. To lament and grieve into a void is one thing; to lament and grieve when God is paying attention to you is another. The passage from Job assures each of us that God attends to our mourning.

Other suggested Old Testament passages recognize suffering principally through their declarations of consolation. Isaiah 25 promises that God is spreading a rich feast for us; at that feast, "the Lord GOD will wipe away the tears from all faces" (v. 8). Similarly, Isaiah 61 promises "to comfort all who mourn; to provide for those who mourn in Zion—to give them a garland instead of ashes, the oil of gladness instead of mourning" (vv. 2–3). There's a steady acknowledgment of mourning, and a promise to turn mourning into flowers and soothing ointment. The text from Lamentations 3 begins with an almost rousing declaration of God's love: "The steadfast love of the LORD never ceases, his mercies never come to an end; they are new every morning; great is your faithfulness" (vv. 22–23). The passage, which seems at first to sit tensively with mourning, insists that love will overcome death. The next verse explicitly connects God's love with the concept of *hope*—hope for the dead person, and hope for those who mourn him: "The LORD is my portion,' says my soul, 'therefore I will hope in him'" (Lamentations 3:24). The bereaved have gathered to mourn someone they love, and if they mourn without hope, they will have only lament and the certainty that they are parted from the friend they love forever. The soul's declaration that "I will hope in" the Lord forces a fissure in that despair.

> "Let your weeping be bitter and your wailing fervent; make your mourning worthy of the departed, for one day, or two, to avoid criticism; then be comforted for your grief."
> —*Sirach 38:17*

The New Testament passages boldly insist that eventually "God will wipe away every tear" (Revelation 7:17). There are sufferings of the present time, but even death cannot finally separate us from the love of God (Romans 8). Perhaps the densest of the suggested passages is the collection of verses from 1 Corinthians 15. There, Paul says that because Jesus has been raised from the dead, we too can be resurrected; eventually our bodies too will be clothed with immortality. At some point in the future, when God has completed God's program of healing, we will all be able to declare, "Where, O death, is your sting?" (1 Corinthians 15:55). Of course, at a funeral, everyone knows where the sting is, because everyone is feeling it. "Sting" is an apt shorthand for the welter of funereal feelings—the sting is not final; the sting will not kill you; but when you are feeling it, the sting is strong. The death is a temporary agony, for both the dead person and the mourner, and the Scripture passages read at funerals want to affirm both the reality and the impermanence of the agony.

The suggested Gospel passages all come from the Gospel of John and, in one way or another, they all promise that people will live forever. They proclaim "that all who see the Son and believe in him may have eternal life; and I will raise them up on the last day" (John 6:40). One of the suggested passages is the story of Jesus raising Lazarus from the dead; it includes the powerful and poetic lines that open the burial liturgy: "I am the resurrection and the life. Those who believe in me, even though they die, will live, and everyone who lives and believes in me will never die" (John 11:25–26). Many of these passages seem to imply that eternal life is given only to people who believe certain things. When people read John 6 or John 11 in and around funerals, I hope, frankly, that their attention is not focused on the question of what their dead beloved needed to believe in order to be resurrected; I hope that people hearing these Gospel passages at a funeral focus on Jesus—Jesus as the one who was resurrected and who can resurrect us.

Job, Lamentations, Isaiah, 1 Corinthians, the Gospel of John: These passages show us that at funerals we need to lament the loss of the one who died, and hope for something better. And we need to do them *both*: hope without lament is an evasion, and lament without hope is despair.

PAUSE AND CONSIDER The Bible includes accounts of many funerals: we read about the burial of Sarah (Genesis 23:1–20), of Miriam (Numbers 20:1), of Aaron (Numbers 20:22–29). One of the most stirring passages depicts the burial of Moses: "So Moses the servant of the LORD died there in the land of Moab, according to the word of the LORD. And he buried him in a valley in the land of Moab, over against Bethpeor: but no man knoweth of his sepulchre unto this day" (Deuteronomy 34:5–6, KJV). These verses depict God as an undertaker, a gravedigger, burying his beloved friend Moses. This is not an image of God one hears often discussed—there are a lot of churches named Church of the Good Shepherd (after Jesus's self-identification as a good shepherd in John 10:11–18), and a lot of hymns that invoke God as friend (they pick up on Jesus's statement to the disciples, in John 15:15: "I do not call you servants . . . but I have called you friends"). But there are not too many churches named Church of the Blessed Gravedigger. Is the image of God as gravedigger surprising? What does the biblical depiction of God burying Moses show us about God? What would your spiritual life be like if at the center of your prayers was this God, who buried the man that scholars have described as "God's best friend"?

Chapter 7

Swimming in Scripture

In a homily on the letter to the Colossians, John Chrysostom, a late fourth- and early fifth-century preacher, advised his congregation to procure Bibles for their own devotional use. Of course they heard the Scriptures in church—they had just that day heard Colossians 3:16–17. But Chrysostom wanted the men and women in his church to also read, study, and pray the Scriptures when they were at home. He urged his congregation to "dive into" the Scriptures—and then, a sentence later, he expanded the image: "Don't simply dive into them. Swim in them."

Over the centuries, Christians have developed an imaginative array of means by which to study and pray the Scriptures—to swim in them. Here are seven.

Lectio Divina

Lectio divina ("holy reading" in Latin) is an ancient mode of praying that helps us hear God speaking to us through the Scriptures. It involves reading a short biblical passage (say, one to six verses) four times, slowly, with spacious pauses in between.

- During the first read-through, ask the Holy Spirit to direct your attention to a short word or phrase that might hold particular meaning for you.

- During the second reading, holding that word or phrase in mind, ask the Holy Spirit what the word or phrase (or perhaps another word or phrase that seems significant in your second reading) holds for you: Why has your attention turned to this particular phrase? How does it speak to a situation in your life? Or, what situation in your community or the world does it point you toward?

- During the third reading, consider whether you wish to offer a particular response to what you're receiving. You might want to say something to God about what you're hearing in this prayer, or you might realize that because of what you're hearing, there's something you wish to do after the prayer concludes (join a protest, make a gesture of kindness toward your husband, forgive your mother yet again, volunteer at the soup kitchen, call a faraway friend).

- During (and after) the fourth reading, simply dwell with God, in the company of whatever you've received. Sometimes that might mean sitting in comfortable (or uncomfortable) silence with God. Sometimes it might mean laughing with God, or raging, or weeping. When you feel the prayer has concluded, say the Lord's Prayer or another favorite prayer, or simply say "Amen."

I like Christine Valters Paintner and Lucy Wynkoop's description of *lectio*: *lectio* is "an invitation to listen deeply to God's voice in scripture and then to allow what we hear to shape our way of being in the world."

Lectio can be modified for group prayer. Consider sharing it in this way:

- Read the passage aloud, once or twice.

- Ask each person to say, with no commentary, the word or phrase that leapt out at him.

- Read the passage again, and ask each person to say, simply and concisely, what he thinks this passage holds for him, or how it connects to his life.

- Read the passage again, and ask each person to share how she thinks she might respond to what she is receiving in the prayer.

- Read the passage again, and sit for a few minutes in silence.

- Wrap up with the Lord's Prayer or a simple "Amen."

You can't practice *lectio divina* formally during a Sunday church service, because each Scripture passage will be read only once. But you can choose to listen to a given passage with the spirit of *lectio*, asking the Holy Spirit to lift out of the reading a word or phrase that you in particular need to hear.

> **PAUSE AND CONSIDER** *Lectio divina* is a prayer practice that
> emphasizes *listening to*, rather than talking to, God. When
> you think of prayer, what place does speaking to God have?
> What place does listening have?

Ignatian Prayer

Another way of praying with Scripture was developed by Catholic monastic leader Ignatius of Loyola—thus, it's usually called **Ignatian prayer**. Like *lectio divina*, Ignatian prayer assumes that we can hear God speaking to us through the Scriptures. Ignatian prayer is best suited to a story from Scripture, whereas *lectio* is equally suited to any Scripture passage. The heart of Ignatian prayer is *vividly imagining* the story in question.

Select the biblical story you'll be praying, and then listen to the story being read aloud. If you're praying this in a group, one person can read the Scripture aloud, slowly, three or four times. If you're praying alone, you can fire up a Scripture-reading app (like Holy Bible from Life.Church), or you can read the passage aloud or silently to yourself several times. As you read or hear the passage, imagine the story. Draw all your senses into the task of imagining the biblical scene—don't imagine just what the story looks like. Imagine, too, what the landscape smells like, how the sand or soil or grass or floor feels to the feet. What's the soundscape—is it noisy or still? Are there birds chirping? People talking? How's the temperature?

After you have thoroughly imagined the scene, find yourself somewhere in the scene. Maybe you become one of the characters in the story—a disciple feeding the 5,000; the hemorrhaging woman, in need of Jesus's healing; a peony or toucan or leopard at the creation of the world—or maybe you're just yourself, somehow transported to the biblical text. Take a few minutes sometimes opaque phrases and words. "Relocated exegesis" is the practice of relocating your Bible reading to a physical place where you don't typically read the Bible; for me, that means anywhere other than my house, my church, or the school where I teach. So you take a Bible to Target, to the county tax office, to your neighborhood playground, to the war memorial down the block, or to the jellyfish tank at the state aquarium, and you read a passage of Scripture there. You can read aloud or silently; you can do this alone or in a group; you can open the Bible at random, you can read one of the passages you heard in church the previous Sunday, or you can thematically match a passage to your location. (I enjoy matching. In fact, I sometimes get carried away trying to demonstrate my cleverness—all spiritual practices are haunted by sin, and the sin that haunts my practice of relocated exegesis is the pride I take in my ability to ingeniously pair place and theme. So once, I read the tale of Sarah's learning she was going to conceive a child at age 90+ at a retirement community. Another time, I took the passages that seventeenth-century New England Puritans used to justify killing Quakers to Boston Common, where there's a great sculpture of one of the Quaker martyrs. Yet another time, I persuaded a group of people from church to join me in reading biblical passages about food at the local grocery store.)

Sometimes, when reading the Bible at the Food Lion or in the retirement community foyer, nothing much happens. But sometimes—because where we read shapes what we can see in the reading—I see something in the text that I would not have seen at home on my couch: different locations make some readings more likely and others less likely. Increasingly, I'm realizing that relocated exegesis can also show me something about the place where I'm reading—when I take Scripture somewhere strange, the Scriptures help me notice aspects of my surroundings I wouldn't have noticed without the Bible in hand.

If you're intrigued by this practice, but freaked out by the idea of *taking a Bible out in public*, don't worry: the discomfort is part of the point. Occasionally, a stranger asks to join my reading; occasionally, I've been asked to leave a location—all that is part of the point too.

> **PAUSE AND CONSIDER** Where might you like to practice relocated exegesis? Think of three places within 20 miles of your home.

Breath Prayer

A simple way to take Scripture into your body is to sit somewhere comfortable, adopt an unfocused gaze or close your eyes, and take slow, deep breaths. As you inhale, hold in mind (that is, say silently to yourself) the first half of a phrase from the Bible, and as you exhale, hold in mind the second half of the phrase. Continue breathing in and out to the words of this verse for ten or fifteen minutes. "[Inhale] The Lord is my shepherd [exhale] I shall not want"—repeat just that. Or "[inhale] For God alone [exhale] my soul in silence waits." "[Inhale] Your life is hid [exhale] with Christ in God" (when I pray those words from Colossians, I change the pronoun from "your" to "my"). "When I'm afraid / I'll trust in you." "It is for freedom / that Christ has set us free." "Hide me under / the shadow of thy wing."

Labyrinth Walking

I live near several labyrinths—a neighbor's front yard boasts a labyrinth made from wine bottles; my friend Sarah has planted a vegetable garden labyrinth; and a parishioner built one at the college two blocks from the church. A labyrinth is, simply,

a shape—"usually," in the words of the Episcopal priest Lauren Artress, "in the form of a circle with a meandering but pur-
poseful path, from the edge to the center and back out again."
Walking a labyrinth is a form of embodied prayer. As Artress
explains, a labyrinth "has only one path, and once we make the
choice to enter it, the path becomes a metaphor for our journey
through life, sending us to the center of the labyrinth and then
back out to the edge on the same path." Next time you walk a
labyrinth, take a Scripture verse with you. Say it over and over,
aloud or in your mind, as you walk into and out of the labyrinth.

Read a Bible Story with a Child

Whether or not you have children (I don't), reading the Bible
with kids can be generative and surprising, because children,
who come to the Bible with different presuppositions than we
do, are apt to see things in the text that we might not.

I like the questions Elizabeth Caldwell proposes that adults discuss with children after reading a Bible story together (you can find these in Caldwell's book *I Wonder: Engaging a Child's Curiosity about the Bible*):

Who is in the story and what happens to them?
What do you think this story is about?
What kind of story is this?
How is this story different from the time and place in which we live?
Why do you think this story is important?
How do you connect with the story or what does this story have to do with your life?

And, my favorite (because it seems to me to most reveal what's at stake in a given biblical text):

When would be a good time to remember this story?

"Irregular and Nonliterary" Practices

In many earlier eras, Christians read their Bibles, but they also used their Bibles—the actual books, the actual objects—in ways that didn't involve reading. They might place a coin inside the book of Ruth (which includes one of the Bible's great seduction scenes) and put the coined Bible under their pillow, expecting this bit of book-magic to give them a dream of the person they'd one day marry. Or, if someone was sick, a family member might fan the pages of the Bible in front of the patient's face, literalizing the common trope that Scripture is (in the words of Thomas Cranmer) "the most healthful medicine," and expecting the act of page-fanning to help the person get well. In the nineteenth century, a woman in Hampshire, England, "ate a New Testament, day by day and leaf by leaf, between two sides of bread and butter, as a remedy for fits." Historian David Cressy has referred to these practices as "irregular" (which is not to say rare) and "nonliterary uses" of the Bible. People put Bibles to work in magical and enchanted ways exactly because they believed Bibles overflowed with meaning; what's in a Bible is so much, so abundant, that it overflows the words of the text.

I don't think of myself as especially superstitious, but in fact I attribute this kind of excessive meaning to objects—meaning beyond the obvious use and function of the object—all the time. I believe that certain material objects have special properties and I want to have the objects around me because of those properties—and the special properties of the objects are inseparable from the person or people the object has been close to. I keep close at hand a green fountain pen with which one of my teachers, now dead, wrote the book he was working on when we met. Whenever I try to actually use a fountain pen, I wind up with giant blobs of ink on my fingers, so typically the pen just sits on my desk. But I like to have it nearby, because it summons my friend, and all his book-writing brilliance. I half-think that just by sitting there, the pen might help me write more like the friend who bequeathed it to me. Similarly, I don't much like my mother's china pattern, but I enjoy using the dishes because they belonged to my mother.

I regret that the "irregular and nonliterary" practices of Bible-as-love-charm, Bible-as-healing-agent—practices that, in the words of historian Paul C. Gutjahr, make clear that Bibles not only "communicate meaning via written symbols," but also, as material objects, "are powerful mediums of communication in and of themselves"—have been largely abandoned by modern Americans as mere superstition. Practices like *lectio divina* and Ignatian prayer foster intimacy with Scripture and with the God of Scripture in part by drawing us into closer contact with the words of Scripture. But I'd like the church to reclaim some of these practices that find abundance not in the verbal content of the Scriptures, but just in the object of the Bible itself. Using my mother's dishes makes me closer to my mother because the dishes were hers; they are of her and from her and close to her. So, too, simply being close to the object that is the Bible can draw us close to the God whose Bible it was first.

PAUSE AND CONSIDER Which of these seven practices of "swimming in Scripture" appeals to you most? Why?

Abundant, Inexhaustible

Recently, I copied out this poem from George Herbert:

> As on a window late I cast mine eye,
> I saw a vine drop grapes with *J* and *C*
> Anneal'd on every bunch. One standing by
> Ask'd what it meant. I, who am never loth
> To spend my judgement, said, It seem'd to me
> To be the bodie and the letters both
> Of *Joy* and *Charitie*. Sir, you have not miss'd,
> The man reply'd; It figures *JESUS CHRIST*.

I love this poem. I love the shadowy man "standing by" (in a trenchcoat, I like to think). I love the narrator's ability to poke fun at himself, acknowledging that he never hesitates to give his opinion. And I love what the poem has to say about letters, and about reading letters.

Most straightforwardly, I suppose, the poem is about Jesus. The speaker of the poem isn't mistaken (hasn't "miss'd") in thinking that the "J" and "C" are shorthand for "Joy" and "Charitie," because the quintessence of joy and charity are found in Jesus Christ—so the letters' figuring Jesus doesn't prevent, and indeed requires, their also figuring charity and joy.

But if the poem is about Jesus, it's also about reading written text. It suggests that a text can mean more than one thing (just as the poem itself means something about Jesus, and something about reading). Every text is inexhaustible; every text means more than its author or its readers think it means. "J"s and "C"s can signify virtues and Jesus, both.

But Scripture is peculiarly inexhaustible. That's part of what Christians indicate when they name Scripture as Scripture, and that's why we keep reading it—because there are always more meanings to find.

And, as the Herbert poem suggests, all those meanings somehow disclose God.

One reason I like this poem is that it includes grapes. I don't know exactly what grapes "anneal'd" (that is, enameled, or fired, as glazed ware is fired) with letters look like, but I enjoy trying to picture it. And I have to think that Herbert wrote about grapes rather than, say, crabapples, because grapes are everywhere in the Bible: they're props in people's harvest celebrations and, in the Song of Songs, they mark the place where the lovers will finally have sex. (Also, sour grapes that set your teeth on edge are used by the prophets as a metaphor for sin.) Grapes, in Scripture, figure the abundant gifts of the Lord—gifts that number among them, of course, Scripture itself. So in Herbert's poem, we can read the grape bunches on which the men spy "J" and "C" as the Bible. Whatever the Bible is saying—whatever it's saying about virtues, whatever it's saying about windows or fruit or trenchcoats—it's also always saying something about Jesus. It's always pointing to God.

Acknowledgments

Many thanks to Stephanie Spellers, who invited me to write *A Word to Live By*, and to Nancy Bryan and the entire team at Church Publishing; to the colleagues and friends who helped me think about the questions pondered in this book—Ellen Davis, Susan Eastman, Sarah Jobe (to whom I owe chapter one's comparison of Bible reading to Jacob's wrestling with the angel), Thea Portier-Young, Warren Smith, Jim Turrell, and Ross Wagner; and to Brian Cole, Stephen Chapman, Ann Gillespie, Paul Griffiths, and Joel Marcus for reading—and then being willing to endlessly discuss—drafts of the book. I'm grateful, also, to the congregation at St. Paul's Episcopal Church in Louisburg, North Carolina, for giving me a place to love the Bible more deeply.

Thank you, thank you, thank you.

Notes

Preface

Page v: Rowan Greer, *Anglican Approaches to Scripture: From the Reformation to the Present* (New York: Crossroad, 2006), xxvi.

Chapter 1

Page 5: Jerome, quoted in Richard Swinbure, *Revelation: From Metaphor to Analogy*, 2nd ed. (New York: Oxford University Press, 2007), 187.

Page 7: Martin Luther quoted in Martin Goodman, "Introduction to the Apocrypha," in John Barton and John Muddiman, eds., *The Oxford Bible Commentary* (New York: Oxford University Press, 2007), 619.

Page 7: *The Canons and Decrees of the Sacred and Oecumenical Council of Trent,* trans. J. Waterworth (London: Doman, 1848), 17.

Page 7: The sixteenth-century Anglican formulation "read for example of life and instruction of manners" can be found in the 1979 edition of the Book of Common Prayer (hereafter cited as "BCP"), 868.

Chapter 2

Page 9: BCP, 211.

Page 10: BCP, 236.

Page 10: Anselm of Canterbury, quoted in Paul J. Griffiths, *Religious Reading: The Place of Reading in the Practice of Religion* (New York: Oxford University Press, 1999), 43.

Page 13: On Job's daughters, see Ellen F. Davis, *Getting Involved with God: Rediscovering the Old Testament* (Lanham, MD: Cowley Publications, 2001), 142.

Chapter 3

Page 21: Gordon D. Free and Douglas Stuart. *How to Read the Bible for All Its Worth*, 4th ed. (Grand Rapids, MI: Zondervan, 2014), 16–20.

Page 24: Stanley Hauerwas and William H. Willimon, *The Truth about God: The Ten Commandments in Christian Life* (Nashville: Abingdon Press, 1999), 20.

Page 26: Athanasius, "The Letter of Athanasius to Marcellinus," quoted in Benjamin Wayman, *Make the Words Your Own: An Early Christian Guide to the Psalms* (Brewster, MA: Paraclete Press, 2014), xv.

Chapter 4

Page 36: Anonymous document about the distribution of religious books, Virginia Miscellany, miscellaneous microfilm reel 19, n.p., Library of Virginia (Richmond).

Page 44: Agobard of Lyon, quoted in Barbara Baert, "The Annunciation and the Senses: *Ruach, Pneuma,* Odour," in Renana Bartal and Hanna Vorholt, eds., *Between Jerusalem and Europe: Essays in Honour of Bianca Kühnel* (Leiden: Brill, 2015), 202.

Chapter 5

Page 47: Hughes Oliphant Old, *Leading in Prayer: A Workbook for Worship* (Grand Rapids, MI: Eerdmans, 1995), 7.

Page 49: For a brilliant exploration of the idea that "Luke . . . depicts the birth as an event that is 'unregistered' in two senses: it is beyond the bounds of the prevailing social context, and it goes unnoticed by most of those around. Jesus is not officially registered, nor do those around him register the fact that his arrival has any significance," and that "It is not that we recognize the birth of Jesus and then sing the Gloria, but that we hear and sing 'Glory to God in the highest' and are thereby enabled to see the entrance of Jesus into our world," see Martha L. Moore-Keish, "Between Text & Sermon: Luke 2:1–14," *Interpretation: A Journal of Bible and Theology* 60.4 (October 2006): 442–44.

Page 53: Sarah Ruhl interviewed by Paula Vogel, *BOMB* 99 (Spring 2007): http://bombmagazine.org/article/2902/sarah-ruhl

Page 54: Catherine Weate, *Modern Voice: Working with Actors on Contemporary Text* (London: Oberon Books, 2012), chapter 5.

Chapter 6

Page 63: Oecumenius, *Commentary on the Apocalypse*, excerpted in William C. Weinrich, ed., *Revelation* (Downers Grove, IL: InterVarsity Press, 2005), 302.

Page 67: For the description of Moses as "God's best friend," see Davis, *Getting Involved with God*, 46.

Chapter 7

Page 69: John Chrysostom, quoted in Christopher A. Hall, *Reading Scripture with the Church Fathers* (Downers Grove, IL: InterVarsity Press, 1998), 96.

Page 71: Christine Valters Paintner and Lucy Wynkoop, *Lectio Divina: Contemplative Awakening and Awareness* (New York: Paulist Press, 2008), 1.

Page 76: Lauren Artress, *Walking a Sacred Path: Rediscovering the Labyrinth as a Spiritual Practice* (New York: Penguin, 2006), xxi–xxii.

Page 77: Elizabeth Caldwell, *I Wonder: Engaging a Child's Curiosity about the Bible* (Nashville: Abingdon Books, 2016).

Page 77: Thomas Cranmer, "A Prologue or Preface to the Holy Bible" (1540), in John Strype, ed., *Memorials of Archbishop Cranmer*, Vol. II (London: George Routledge and Co., 1853), 488.

Page 77: For love-charms and healing arts, as well as the woman from Hampshire, see David Cressy, "Books as Totems in Seventeenth-Century England and New England," *Journal of Library History* 21:1 (Winter 1986), 92–106.

Page 78: Paul C. Gutjahr, *An American Bible: A History of the Good Book in the United States*, 1777–1880 (Stanford: Stanford University Press, 1999), 41.

Conclusion

Page 81: George Herbert, "Love-joy," in Helen Wilcox, *The English Poems of George Herbert* (Cambridge: Cambridge University Press), 413–15.